Mr. Franklin

BENJAMIN FRANKLIN
Terra cotta bust by Jean Jacques Caffieri, 1777

Mr Franklin

A SELECTION

FROM HIS PERSONAL LETTERS

Edited by Leonard W. Labaree and Whitfield J. Bell, Jr.

Benjamin Franklin

New Haven: Yale University Press

London: Geoffrey Cumberlege, Oxford University Press

1956

E
302.6
F75
A 195

First published, January, 1956
Second printing, January, 1956

Library of Congress catalog card number 56-5026

Printed in the United States of America

36552

This volume is published January 17, 1956,

to commemorate the two hundred and fiftieth anniversary

of the birth of Benjamin Franklin.

The letters presented here are selected from

THE PAPERS OF BENJAMIN FRANKLIN,

a work in progress under the auspices of

the American Philosophical Society

and Yale University

CONTENTS

ILLUSTRATIONS

INTRODUCTION

ON January 17, 1706, as we reckon the calendar today, the wife of a candle-maker of Boston, Josiah Franklin, presented to him his fifteenth child and tenth son. The parents named him Benjamin after the father's youngest brother. Following a brief schooling the boy was put out to learn the printer's trade, but a few years later he ran away to Philadelphia. There he became a prosperous printer and publisher; then, retiring from active business, he devoted his attention in turn to scientific investigation, provincial and imperial politics, and diplomacy. In each of these three fields he won renown on two continents; he was honored by colleges, universities, and learned societies at home and abroad and was entertained by nobles and churchmen, by courtiers and kings. When he died at the age of eighty-four he was mourned as one of the great men of the world. Twenty thousand people, the greatest assemblage Philadelphia had ever seen, watched his funeral procession. The members of the American House of Representatives and the French National Assembly voted unanimously to wear mourning for this man who had begun life as the youngest son of a simple artisan in the provincial town of Boston. These, in briefest outline, are the basic facts in the career of one of the outstanding men in our history, the two hundred and fiftieth anniversary of whose birth is being celebrated on January 17, 1956.

Franklin's life, nearly spanning the eighteenth century, saw the rise of the American people from colonial subordination and intense localism to political independence and national union, from crude frontier provincialism to a cultural maturity of substantial achievements and great promise for the future. In nearly every phase of this evolution and growth Benjamin Franklin was a central figure, so central, in fact, that there is more than a little justification for calling his period "The Age of Franklin."

This is not the place to analyze in detail the elements of Franklin's greatness, if indeed it is ever possible to analyze satisfactorily a man of authentic genius. But certain facts stand out clearly. His was an extraordinarily versatile personality. He was a journalist, scientist, author, and inventor; a civic leader, postal administrator, politician, and diplomat; a wit, philosopher, and statesman; an enthusiastic and expert swimmer and—charmingly—a flirtatious septuagenarian. Printers still regard him as their patron saint. He is a symbol to the bankers who promote National Thrift Week. And he was, as David Hume rightly declared, the first great man of letters for whom Europe was beholden to America.

Franklin was, in short, a well-rounded man, of broad knowledge and understanding. Almost wholly self-educated, he was insatiably curious on nearly every topic of importance in his day. He taught himself several foreign languages and read widely and avidly both the works of standard authors of the past and the significant writings of his own contemporaries. An English correspondent had standing instructions to send him regularly "such new Pamphlets as are worth reading on any Subject (Religious Controversy excepted)" just as soon as they were published in London. The habit of reading, of wide and thoughtful reading, stayed with him to the very end. His education—a lifelong process—was as broad and as liberal as he could make it.

Franklin was not only a reader of varied and catholic tastes; he was a writer too. Prose writing, he asserted in a well-known passage in his memoirs, had been of great use to him in the course of his life; his mastery of a good English style was "a principal means" of his advancement. Certainly no American of his day wrote more effectively, with such apparent ease, as the letters in this selection demonstrate. Whether he described a scientific experiment, recorded his conversation with a child in a coach returning to London, or proposed a way to pay the costs of war, Franklin wrote simply and aptly. Everything that came from his pen met his own requirements of good writing, that it be smooth, clear, and short.

Franklin's letters are good reading; they also reveal him again in all his astonishing many-sidedness. On a single day—August 22, 1772—he wrote at least thirteen letters to as many persons on subjects as different as canals, antislavery propaganda, obtaining workmen for a glass factory, oath taking, post office accounts, silk culture, business conditions, the selection of books for the Library Company, the establishment of a nailery, and the Pennsylvania Hospital's English investments.

The moods of his letters are as varied as the subjects: condescension toward a younger sister, angry indignation at the enemies of his country, unruffled confidence that truth is mighty and will prevail. Franklin can be biting when he must; witness his letter to Jeremiah Meyer. Explaining to a niece "that matter" of the kindnesses of the French women to him, he is urbane, seeming to leave so much unsaid. And few readers are likely to be unmoved by the warmth and depth of feeling in his farewell to David Hartley. This variety of mood is as striking as Franklin's all-embracing interest and achievement and is equally a reason why Carl Van Doren described him as "a harmonious human multitude."

For all these reasons letters of Benjamin Franklin have been printed and reprinted repeatedly during and since his lifetime. His English scientific friend Peter Collinson brought out in 1751 a collection of his communications on electrical investigations under the title *Experiments and Observations on Electricity*. His French correspondent Dubourg published a selection from Franklin's more miscellaneous letters and papers in 1773. His English admirer Benjamin Vaughan did likewise in 1779—an interesting commentary both on the extent of Franklin's reputation in England even during the American Revolution and on the political tolerance of the time. Since Franklin's death in 1790 four general editions of his letters and other papers have appeared. The first of these was prepared by his grandson William Temple Franklin and was published in six volumes, 1817–1818. The most recent, Albert Henry Smyth's ten-volume edition, drew on all its predecessors and uncovered new materials as well. Published 1905–1907, it was one of the lasting achievements of the elaborate, far-flung Franklin bicentennial celebration. All this while and in the half century since the Smyth edition, innumerable selections from Franklin's correspondence were being made and published. Some appeared in small collections like the present work; others in larger but still limited anthologies; again, individual letters of particular interest were printed, sometimes in periodicals, often separately and handsomely as keepsakes.

Now another general edition of Franklin's writings is in preparation. It was announced on Franklin's birthday in 1954 by the American Philosophical Society and Yale University. The editorial costs are being financed by a generous gift to Yale University from Time, Inc., on behalf of Life Magazine, and by grants from the American Philosophical Society. The partnership of the two institutions is fitting. The Society, which Franklin founded, owns more than 15,000 of his papers (more than half of all known to exist) and for some years has been spending large sums in expanding its manuscript holdings and in financing Franklin research. In the Franklin Collection given to Yale some twenty years ago by William Smith Mason the University possesses the outstanding collection of printed material by and about Franklin and his period. The Yale University Press will publish the new edition.

The work now in preparation will contain everything Franklin wrote that can be found and, for the first time, in full or in abstract, all letters addressed to him. Reaching to at least twenty-five volumes, it will supersede all previous editions, for hundreds of letters by Franklin have turned up since Smyth's edition of fifty years ago and no previous edition has contained any significant number of letters to Franklin. Only by giving the whole of his two-way correspondence—the letters his friends and associates wrote to him as well as those he wrote to them—is it possible to present adequately the thought and activity of the man.

Material for this edition is now being actively gathered from all over the world into a central file of photostatic copies. The papers are widely scattered and the search is requiring years, rather than merely months. In one sense it can never be complete, for many of Franklin's papers have not survived. An unknown number were destroyed during the American Revolution in the sacking of a friend's house, where Franklin had left them for safekeeping. His grandson and first general editor, to whom he bequeathed his books and papers, was at best careless of them. Years after William Temple Franklin had finished using them for his edition some turned up on the shelf of a London tailor's shop; a large block of papers remained for fifty years in the garret of a Philadelphia stable. These manuscripts are now safely housed in major libraries. Some of Franklin's correspondents carefully preserved the letters he wrote to them; others generously gave away his autograph letters as souvenirs. Six institutions—the American Philosophical Society, the Library of Congress, the Historical Society of Pennsylvania, the National Archives, the University of Pennsylvania, and Yale University—together own about four-fifths of the existing Franklin manuscripts. The remainder—perhaps five or six thousand pieces—are widely scattered, held by scores of libraries, large and small, and by dozens of individuals in the United States, Great Britain, and Continental Europe. The editors of THE PAPERS OF BENJAMIN FRANKLIN are seeking the cooperation of all these owners to allow the inclusion of the letters they hold in the forthcoming edition. Thus far these institutions and individuals have been most generous, but it is not easy to find them all. The editors hope that any reader of these lines who knows the location of a Franklin document will inform them of its whereabouts, for any edition of his writings, as one well-wisher told another editor a century ago, may properly be considered in some sense "a national work."

The present book is not in that sense "a national work." It would have been gratifying and appropriate if the first volume of the projected comprehensive PAPERS OF BENJAMIN FRANKLIN could have been published in time to mark the two hundred and fiftieth anniversary of Franklin's birth on January 17, 1956. This could not be, for even the task of searching out and assembling the material is still incomplete and the major editorial preparation is still to come. Yet the sponsors, publishers, and editors of THE PAPERS could not omit their particular birthday tribute: hence this selection of Franklin's letters. It has been prepared not for Franklin specialists or historical scholars but for all Americans who treasure this nation's past and would like to know a little better one of the founders of the Republic.

Our aim, very simply, is to re-introduce Benjamin Franklin, the man, to his fellow citizens of the middle of the twentieth century. The two dozen or so letters we present here are personal. None of the state papers is included. The Pennsylvania politician, the imperial statesman, the diplomatist need the broader canvas the forthcoming comprehensive edition will provide. Even Franklin's printing and scientific interests receive less space here than they deserve. We have chosen these letters to illustrate, as much as can be done in these few pages, the richness of his personality, the variety of his interests and activities, the warmth of his human relationships, and something of his attitude toward life. It is by presenting Franklin the human being in his own words, as he addressed them informally to relatives, friends, and associates, that we would mark the anniversary of his birth.

We have not insisted that each letter be hitherto unpublished. Where we found a good unpublished letter among the manuscripts we have so far examined, we chose it, of course, gladly; but we have not hesitated to print what has been printed before, even many times before, if we felt that it best suited our particular purpose. Most of these letters, in fact, have been printed in one place or another, although sometimes only in publications of very limited circulation; more than a quarter of them are not to be found in any of the previous general editions. Whenever possible we have drawn our text from an original manuscript; when such has not survived we have used the earliest printed version, sometimes one which appeared during Franklin's own lifetime.

We are presenting this selection of letters with only what seemed needed for each by way of introduction and with none of the scholarly apparatus of annotation, collation, and bibliography which the comprehensive edition will have. We have retained the spelling, capitalization, and punctuation of the originals—Franklin was a printer and had very firm opinions on how manuscripts should be rendered into type—except that we have spelled out abbreviations acceptable in his day but no longer familiar. The only other liberties we have taken with the texts have been to omit with proper indication certain sentences in one letter which were not needed in the context and which would have added unnecessary length and required cumbersome explanation, to add quotation marks where needed within another, and in two other letters to drop without specific indication postscripts on somewhat irrelevant matters.

The Table of Contents and the List of Illustrations indicate in each instance the location of the original which we have used. To these various owners, both private individuals and institutions, we are deeply grateful for permission to share their treasures with a wider circle of readers. The courtesy and the cooperation they have shown us are characteristic of all those who are making available the material for the comprehensive edition we are preparing. At the appropriate time and place the contributions of each of this much larger group will be formally and gratefully acknowledged.

Meanwhile, on this anniversary of his birth we are simply presenting Mr. Franklin—Deborah's husband, Sally's father, the generous counselor, the warm friend, the entertaining correspondent. This is a glimpse of Franklin the man, in all the colorful variety of his experience and feeling, the one above all Americans who combined most happily the greatest talents and the greatest human attractiveness.

A BRIEF CHRONOLOGY OF BENJAMIN FRANKLIN

1706   January 17 (January 6, 1705, by "Old Style" reckoning). Born in Boston, the youngest son of Josiah and Abiah (Folger) Franklin

1718   Apprenticed to his brother James, a printer

1723   Runs away from his apprenticeship, goes to New York and then to Philadelphia, where he gains employment as a printer

1724–26   In London, working as a printer. Back to Philadelphia in October 1726

1728   Forms first printing partnership in Philadelphia

1730   Takes to wife Deborah (Read) Rogers (September 1)

1732   Publishes first issue of *Poor Richard's Almanack* (for year 1733)

1746   Begins electrical experiments

1747   Retires from active business, turning over management of Philadelphia printing establishment to partner David Hall

1751   His letters on electricity brought out in London by his friend Peter Collinson as a pamphlet or book under the title *Experiments and Observations on Electricity*

1753   Harvard and Yale confer honorary degree of Master of Arts upon him. The Royal Society (London) awards him the Sir Godfrey Copley gold medal for his electrical experiments. Appointed joint Deputy Postmaster General of North America

1754   Proposes a plan of colonial union at Albany Congress

1757–62   In England as agent for Pennsylvania Assembly

1759   Receives honorary degree of Doctor of Laws from the University of St. Andrews, Scotland

1764–75   In England as agent for Pennsylvania Assembly (for the second time), serving part of the time also as agent for Georgia, New Jersey, and Massachusetts

1766   Examined in House of Commons in support of repeal of the
        Stamp Act

1774   Examined (and berated) before Privy Council by Solicitor Gen-
        eral Wedderburn on activities as Massachusetts agent. Dis-
        missed from office as Deputy Postmaster General of North
        America. Wife dies (December 19)

1775   The day after arrival in Philadelphia (May 5) is elected delegate
        of Pennsylvania to Second Continental Congress. Serves also
        as chairman of Pennsylvania Committee of Safety

1776   Presides over Constitutional Convention of Pennsylvania. One
        of a committee of five to draft the Declaration of Independ-
        ence. Arrives in Paris (December 21) as one of Commissioners
        of Congress to the French Court

1778   Signs French Alliance (February 6) and Treaty of Commerce
        with France. Appointed by Congress (September 14) sole
        Minister Plenipotentiary of the United States to France

1782   Signs preliminary Treaty of Peace with Great Britain
        (November 30)

1783   Signs definitive Treaty of Peace with Great Britain (September 3).
        Both peace treaties signed by Franklin as one of the American
        Commissioners to Negotiate Peace

1785   Lands at Philadelphia (September 14) on last return to America.
        Elected President of the Supreme Executive Council of Penn-
        sylvania (October 18), serving three years

1787   Attends Federal Constitutional Convention as delegate from
        Pennsylvania

1790   April 17. Dies at his home in Philadelphia, aged 84 years,
        4 months.

Mr. Franklin

BENJAMIN was the fifteenth of his father's seventeen children, the last of his ten sons; but he was first in success and worldly goods. Cheerfully, as his means allowed, Benjamin accepted his responsibilities for the others. To brothers and sisters, then to nieces and nephews, ultimately to grandnieces and grandnephews in the bewildering Franklin genealogy he gave advice and encouragement. He threw business their way, got them appointments in the Post Office which he headed, lent them money and made them allowances when they were old and sick, and provided for them in his wills. With his youngest sister Jane the sense of obligation was less important than genuine affection and the capacity of each to share the other's thoughts and experience. This earliest surviving letter to her was occasioned by news of her impending marriage, at the age of fifteen, to Edward Mecom of Boston. If the tone of big brother's letter is a little condescending, that is perhaps to be excused; he was, after all, twenty-one years old and had been making his own way in the world for more than three years.

To Jane Franklin

Philadelphia, January 6, 1726–7

Dear Sister,

I am highly pleased with the account captain Freeman gives me of you. I always judged by your behaviour when a child that you would make a good, agreeable woman, and you know you were ever my peculiar favourite. I have been thinking what would be a suitable present for me to make, and for you to receive, as I hear you are grown a celebrated beauty. I had almost determined on a tea table, but when I considered that the character of a good housewife was far preferable to that of being only a pretty gentlewoman, I concluded to send you a *spinning wheel*, which I hope you will accept as a small token of my sincere love and affection.

3

Sister, farewell, and remember that modesty, as it makes the most homely virgin amiable and charming, so the want of it infallibly renders the most perfect beauty disagreeable and odious. But when that brightest of female virtues shines among other perfections of body and mind in the same person, it makes the woman more lovely than an angel. Excuse this freedom, and use the same with me. I am, dear Jenny,

Your loving brother,
B. Franklin

THE SCIENTIFIC SPIRIT

PETER COLLINSON, a London Quaker merchant who was agent for several Philadelphia institutions, sent the Library Company in 1746 a glass tube of the kind "philosophers" were using in electrical experiments. Franklin and several friends immediately began to make experiments of their own, observed some phenomena they thought new, and communicated these observations to the learned in England in the form of letters, mostly addressed to Collinson. The merchant read Franklin's letters to the Royal Society and offered them to the editor of the *Gentleman's Magazine* for publication. Some of these letters appeared in London in 1751 as a pamphlet entitled *Experiments and Observations on Electricity, made at Philadelphia in America.* This work, together with its supplements, later editions, and foreign translations, firmly established Franklin's reputation throughout Europe as a scientist. Two personal letters to Collinson, both written in the first months of Franklin's career as an "electrician" but neither included in the earliest editions of this memorable book, suggest better than more formal communications could both the fascinated wonder of Franklin and his circle at the phenomena they were observing for the first time, and the humility of a scientist who would study nature and derive her laws.

Philad Jan. 27. 1746/7

I receiv'd yours of the 26th past, which
I shall endeavour to answer fully per next Post.
In the mean time please to tender my best Respects & Service to good Mr & Mrs Noyes,
and the most agreable Ladies their Daughters,
with Thanks for the Civility they were pleased
to shew me when at Newhaven. — We
have printed nothing new here lately, except
the Enclos'd Pamphlet, which I send, in hope
it may afford the Ladies & yourself some A-
musement these long cold Winter Evenings.
I am, Sir,

Your most humble Servt

B Franklin

FRANKLIN'S PENMANSHIP
A letter to Thomas Darling of New Haven (reduced facsimile)

To Peter Collinson

Philadelphia, March 28, 1747

Sir,

Your kind present of an electric tube, with directions for using it, has put several of us on making electrical experiments, in which we have observed some particular phaenomena that we look upon to be new. I shall, therefore communicate them to you in my next, though possibly, they may not be new to you, as among the numbers daily employed in those experiments on your side the water, 'tis probable some one or other has hit on the same observations. For my own part, I never was before engaged in any study that so totally engrossed my attention and my time as this has lately done; for what with making experiments when I can be alone, and repeating them to my Friends and Acquaintance, who, from the novelty of the thing, come continually in crouds to see them, I have, during some months past, had little leisure for any thing else.

I am, etc.

B. Franklin

To Peter Collinson

Philadelphia, August 14, 1747

Sir

I have lately written two long Letters to you on the Subject of Electricity, one by the Governors Vessel, the other per Mesnard. On some further Experiments since, I have observ'd a Phenomenon or two that I cannot at present account for on the Principles laid down in those Letters, and am therefore become a little diffident of my Hypothesis, and asham'd that I have express'd myself in so positive a manner. In going on with these Experiments, how many pretty Systems do we build, which we soon find ourselves oblig'd to destroy! If there is no other Use discover'd of Electricity, this, however, is something considerable, that it may *help to make a vain Man humble*. I must now request that you would not expose those Letters; or if you communicate them to any Friends, you would at least conceal my Name. I have not Time to add, but that I am, Sir,

Your obliged and most humble Servant

B. Franklin

FAMILY REPORT

FRANKLIN lived too far away from his parents and his numerous brothers and sisters in New England for all of them to keep in close touch with each other in those days of slow and difficult communication. Yet they did exchange letters at irregular intervals and usually took the opportunity, when writing, to pass along recent family news. One such letter to his mother Abiah Franklin, then eighty-three and a widow for the past five years, gives a glimpse of her youngest son's Philadelphia household during that short, happy interval between his retirement from active business as a printer and his full immersion in public affairs. Comments on the perennial servant problem—this time, misbehaving Negro slaves—and news of other relatives recently moved to Philadelphia accompany reports on his children and himself: William, who had been on the Canadian military expedition a few years before and was only just settling down again; and little Sarah (or Sally), "going on seven," who, throughout his life, was her father's special joy. His contentment with life, during this rare period of creative leisure, is fully apparent.

To Abiah Franklin

Honoured Mother

We received your kind Letter of the 2d Instant, and are glad to hear you still enjoy such a Measure of Health, notwithstanding your great Age. We read your Writing very easily; I never met with a Word in your Letters but what I could readily understand; for tho' the Hand is not always the best, the Sense makes every thing plain.

My Leg, which you enquire after, is now quite well. I still keep those Servants, but the Man not in my own House; I have hired him out to the Man that takes Care of my Dutch Printing Office, who agrees to keep him in Victuals and Clothes, and to pay me a Dollar a Week for his Work. His Wife since that Affair behaves exceeding well: But we conclude to sell them both the first good Opportunity; for we do not like Negro Servants. We got again about half what we lost.

As to your Grandchildren, Will. is now 19 Years of Age, a tall proper Youth, and much of a Beau. He acquir'd a Habit of Idleness on the Expedition, but begins of late to apply himself to Business, and I hope will become an industrious Man. He imagin'd his Father had got enough for him: But I have assur'd him that I intend to spend what little I have, myself; if it please God that I live long enough: And as he by no means wants Sense, he can see by my going on, that I am like to be as good as my Word.

Sally grows a fine Girl, and is extreamly industrious with her Needle, and delights in her Book. She is of a most affectionate Temper, and perfectly Dutiful and obliging, to her Parents and to all. Perhaps I flatter my self too much; but I have Hopes that she will prove an ingenious sensible notable and worthy Woman, like her Aunt Jenney. She goes now to the Dancing School.

For my own Part, at present I pass my time agreeably enough. I enjoy (thro' Mercy) a tolerable Share of Health; I read a great deal, ride a little; do a little Business for my self, more for others; retire when I can, and go [into] Company when I please; so the Years roll round, and the last will come; when I would rather have it said, *He lived usefully*, than, *He died rich*.

Cousins Josiah and Sally are well, and I believe will do well, for they are an industrious saving young Couple: But they want a little more Stock to go on smoothly with their Business.

My love to Brother and Sister Mecom and their Children, and to all my Relations in general. I am   Your dutiful Son

B. Franklin

A WHIRLWIND FOR MR. FRANKLIN

EVERY man's conduct provided Franklin with the data of morality and politics. Similarly he found the data of science everywhere. Because his eye was accurate and his words precise, Franklin made daily occurrences seem the prototypes of the grand and timeless. A wind gust swirling up the road was to most travelers only an annoyance that irritated their eyes and frightened their horses; but to Franklin it was a phenomenon to be observed, experimented on, recorded, and communicated to his fellow philosophers. Peter Collinson, an English merchant and naturalist, was for many years Franklin's most regular scientific correspondent in the mother country.

To Peter Collinson

Philadelphia, August 25, 1755

Dear Sir,

As you have my former papers on Whirlwinds, etc. I now send you an account of one which I had lately an opportunity of seeing and examining myself.

8

Being in Maryland, riding with Col. Tasker, and some other gentlemen to his country-seat, where I and my son were entertained by that amiable and worthy man, with great hospitality and kindness, we saw in the vale below us, a small whirlwind beginning in the road, and shewing itself by the dust it raised and contained. It appeared in the form of a sugar-loaf, spinning on its point, moving up the hill towards us, and enlarging as it came forward. When it passed by us, its smaller part near the ground, appeared not bigger than a common barrel, but widening upwards, it seemed, at 40 or 50 feet high, to be 20 or 30 feet in diameter. The rest of the company stood looking after it, but my curiosity being stronger, I followed it, riding close by its side, and observed its licking up, in its progress, all the dust that was under its smaller part. As it is a common opinion that a shot, fired through a waterspout, will break it, I tried to break this little whirlwind, by striking my whip frequently through it, but without any effect. Soon after, it quitted the road and took into the woods, growing every moment larger and stronger, raising, instead of dust, the old dry leaves with which the ground was thick covered, and making a great noise with them and the branches of the trees, bending some tall trees round in a circle swiftly and very surprizingly, though the progressive motion of the whirl was not so swift but that a man on foot might have kept pace with it, but the circular motion was amazingly rapid. By the leaves it was now filled with, I could plainly perceive that the current of air they were driven by, moved upwards in a spiral line; and when I saw the trunks and bodies of large trees invelop'd in the passing whirl, which continued intire after it had left them, I no longer wondered that my whip had no effect on it in its smaller state. I accompanied it about three quarters of a mile, till some limbs of dead trees, broken off by the whirl, flying about, and falling near me, made me more apprehensive of danger; and then I stopped, looking at the top of it as it went on, which was visible, by means of the leaves contained in it, for a very great height above the trees. Many of the leaves, as they got loose from the upper and widest

9

part, were scattered in the wind; but so great was their height in the air, that they appeared no bigger than flies. My son, who was, by this time, come up with me, followed the whirlwind till it left the woods, and crossed an old tobacco-field, where, finding neither dust nor leaves to take up, it gradually became invisible below as it went away over that field. The course of the general wind then blowing was along with us as we travelled, and the progressive motion of the whirlwind was in a direction nearly opposite, though it did not keep a strait line, nor was its progressive motion uniform, it making little sallies on either hand as it went, proceeding sometimes faster, and sometimes slower, and seeming sometimes for a few seconds almost stationary, then starting forwards pretty fast again. When we rejoined the company, they were admiring the vast height of the leaves, now brought by the common wind, over our heads. These leaves accompanied us as we travelled, some falling now and then round about us, and some not reaching the ground till we had gone near three miles from the place where we first saw the whirlwind begin. Upon my asking Col. Tasker if such whirlwinds were common in Maryland, he answered pleasantly, *No, not at all common; but we got this on purpose to treat* Mr. Franklin. And a very high treat it was, to

Dear Sir,

Your affectionate friend,

and humble servant

B. F[ranklin]

_____

A PHILOSOPHER LOOKS AT DEATH

WHILE he was not a professing member of any Christian sect or denomination, Franklin carried with him through life a firm belief in the reality of God, in His benevolent concern in the affairs of men, and in the immortality of the human spirit. Religion was not a regular topic of his correspondence, but he had no hesitation in discussing his convictions on any suitable occasion. He seems to have expressed his religious sentiments most freely of all to friends and relatives in New England, as if he felt that people in that section would be most likely to expect such utterances and would read his words with greatest sympathy and approval. One of the occasions on which he put his beliefs on paper followed the death of his brother John Franklin of Boston in 1756. On receiving the news in Philadelphia he wrote at once to his sister Jane Mecom and then, a few days later, to Elizabeth Hubbard, his brother's young stepdaughter.

To Elizabeth Hubbard

Philadelphia, February 22, 1756

Dear Child,

I condole with you, we have lost a most dear and valuable relation, but it is the will of God and Nature that these mortal bodies be laid aside, when the soul is to enter into real life; 'tis rather an embrio state, a preparation for living: a man is not completely born until he be dead: Why then should we grieve that a new child is born among the immortals? A new member added to their happy society? We are spirits. That bodies should be lent us, while they can afford us pleasure, assist us in acquiring knowledge, or doing good to our fellow creatures, is a kind and benevolent act of God. When they become unfit for these purposes and afford us pain instead of pleasure —instead of an aid, become an incumbrance and answer none of the intentions for which they were given, it is equally kind and benevolent that a way is provided by which we may get rid of them. Death is that way. We ourselves prudently choose a partial death. In some cases a mangled painful limb, which cannot be restored, we willingly cut off. He who plucks out a tooth, parts with it freely since the pain goes with it, and he that quits the whole body, parts at once with all pains and possibilities of pains and diseases it was liable to, or capable of making him suffer.

Our friend and we are invited abroad on a party of pleasure—that is to last forever. His chair was first ready and he is gone before us. We could not all conveniently start together, and why should you and I be grieved at this, since we are soon to follow, and we know where to find him.

Adieu.

B. F[ranklin]

═══════

A LESSON IN RELATIVITY

Helped perhaps by Franklin's letter of sympathy, Bess Hubbard soon recovered her spirits after the death of her stepfather. Eleven months later she wrote her uncle a letter, now lost, to regale him with some amusing story she had heard. Apparently it dealt with the romantic behavior of an elderly person and seemed funnier to the young woman than it did to Franklin, who was just about to celebrate his fifty-first birthday.

To Elizabeth Hubbard

Philadelphia, January 13, 1757

Dear Bess

Your Story is well told and entertaining. Only let me admonish you of a small tho' common Fault of Story-tellers. You should not have introduc'd it by telling me *how comical* it was, especially a Post before you sent the Story it self: For when the Expectation is raised too high, 'tis a Disadvantage to the Thing expected.

But let us not be merely entertain'd by the Tale; let us draw a small Moral from it. Old Age, we see, is subject to Love and its Follies as well as Youth. All old People have been young, and when they were so, they laugh'd, as we do, at the Amours of Age. They imagin'd, 'tis like, that the Case would never be theirs. Let us spare 'em, then; lest the same Case should one day be ours. I see you begin to laugh already at my ranking myself among the

Young! But you, my Girl, when you arrive at Fifty, will think no more of being old, than does   Your affectionate Uncle

                                                                                    B. Franklin

My Love to your good Mama, and to Suky, with
my Thanks for her Care of you in your Illness.
Tell her I now forgive her for selling her Good Luck.

======

TYPE FOR THE CONNOISSEUR

"ONCE a printer, always a printer" is a generalization to which there may be exceptions, but Franklin was not one of them. Although he retired from the active management of his printing office in 1747, signing a contract with his partner David Hall for a share of the profits for eighteen years, he never lost his interest and pride in the craft through which he had made his start in life. During his years in England and France he observed closely the developments in the printer's art and found opportunities to get to know the leading type designers and founders, paper makers, and printers in those countries. In France he established a small press of his own at his home in Passy and found occasional relaxation in setting type himself. His last will, written in 1788, opens proudly with the words: "I, Benjamin Franklin, of Philadelphia, printer."

William Caslon has been commonly regarded as the leading designer and founder of type in England in the eighteenth century. He was rivaled in his day only by John Baskerville, a younger man, whose edition of Virgil, published in 1757, produced something of a sensation and was admired by many connoisseurs, including Franklin. The more ardent devotees of Caslon, however, found much to criticize in Baskerville's types. Upon one such opinionated critic Franklin played a harmless but celebrated trick.

To John Baskerville

Dear Sir,

Let me give you a pleasant Instance of the Prejudice some have entertained against your Work. Soon after I returned, discoursing with a Gentleman concerning the Artists of Birmingham, he said you would [be] a Means of blinding all the Readers in the Nation; for the Strokes of your Letters, being too thin and narrow, hurt the Eye, and he could never read a Line of them without Pain. I thought, said I, you were going to complain of the Gloss of the Paper, some object to. No, no, says he, I have heard that mentioned, but it is not that; it Is in the Form and Cut of the Letters themselves; they have not that Height and Thickness of the Stroke, which make the common Printing so much the more comfortable to the Eye. You see this Gentleman was a Connoisseur. In vain I endeavoured to support your Character against the Charge; he knew what he felt, and could see the Reason of it, and several other Gentlemen among his Friends had made the same Observation, etc. Yesterday he called to visit me, when, mischievously bent to try his Judgment, I stept into my Closet, tore off the Top of Mr. Caslon's specimen, and produced it to him as yours brought with me from Birmingham; saying, I had been examining it, since he spoke to me, and could not for my Life perceive the Disproportion he mentioned, desiring him to point it out to me. He readily undertook it, and went over the several Founts, shewing me every where what he thought Instances of that Disproportion; and declared, that he could not then read the Specimen, without feeling very strongly the Pain he had mentioned to me. I spared him that Time, the Confusion of being told, that these were the Types, he had been reading all his life with so much Ease to his Eyes; the Types his adored Newton is printed with, in which he has pored not a little; nay, the very Types his own Book is printed with, for he is himself an Author, and yet never discovered this painful Disproportion in them, till he thought they were yours. I am, etc.

B. Franklin

AN OPTIMIST AND HIS ENEMIES

EVERY man in public life must expect criticism and even abuse at some stages of his career. One difference among such men is to be found in how they accept these attacks and how they inwardly react to outward enemies. Franklin was no more immune to verbal assaults and false accusations than any of his contemporaries or successors in politics. Some of his American enemies, for example, sought unjustly to lay on his shoulders responsibility for the passage of the Stamp Act and to put upon his actions in that situation the worst possible interpretation. His sister, Mrs. Mecom, was deeply troubled by these attacks and wrote him a pessimistic letter about the state of the world in which such things could happen. His reply, written when he was sixty-one, expresses a characteristic attitude. He could hit back hard and tellingly when the occasion required, but he could treat personal attacks with philosophic calm.

To Jane Mecom

London, March 2, 1767

Dear Sister

I received your kind Letter of Nov. 8. for which I thank you. It rejoices me to hear that you and your Children continue well. I thank God that I too enjoy a greater Share of Health, Strength and Activity than is common with People of my Years, being now Threescore and one. You mention my Opinion of this being a good sort of World, in which you differ from me. Every one should speak as they find. Hitherto I have found it so, and I should be ungrateful to Providence if I did not own it. As to the Abuses I meet with, which you bring as an Argument against my Opinion, you must know I number them among my Honours. One cannot behave so as to obtain the Esteem of the Wise and Good, without drawing on one's self at the same time the Envy and Malice of the Foolish and Wicked, and the latter is a Testimony of the former. The best Men have always had their Share of this Treatment, and the more of it is in proportion to their different and greater degrees of Merit. A Man has therefore some Reason to be asham'd of himself when he meets with none of it. And the World is not to be condemn'd in the Lump because some bad People live in it. Their Number is not great, the Hurt they do is but small, as real good Characters always finally surmount and are established, notwithstanding these Attempts to keep them down. And in the mean time such Enemies do a Man some good, while they think they are doing him harm, by fortifying the Character they would destroy; for when he sees how readily imaginary Faults and Crimes are laid to his Charge, he must be more apprehensive of the Danger of committing real Ones, as he can expect no Quarter, and therefore is more on his Guard to avoid or [at] least to conceal them. So, my dear Sister, when you meet with any more such Letters as that you mention, don't let them give you the least Uneasiness; but call to mind what your Friend good Mr. Whitefield said to me once on such an Occasion: "I read the Libels writ against you, says he, when I was in a remote Province, where I could not be inform'd of the Truth of the Facts; but they rather gave me this good Opinion of you *that you continued to be* USEFUL *to the Publick:* For when I am on the Road, and see Boys in a Field at a Distance, pelting a Tree, though I am too far off to know what Tree it is, I conclude it has FRUIT on it."

I send you per Capt. Freeman a little Box containing some few Articles of Millenery, which Mrs. Stevenson [Franklin's landlady] has bought for you. Her Letter enclos'd will inform you what they are. Be so good as to

16

accept them from me as the Beginning of a little Stock, which if sold to Advantage after being made up by your good Girls, may by Degrees become greater—for on your remitting the Produce to Mrs. Stevenson, she will always readily buy more for you, till by the repeated and accumulated Profits, the Girls grow rich. They may think it a very small beginning. But let them know 'tis more than I had to begin the World with; and that Industry and Frugality early practis'd and long persisted in, will do Wonders. My love to them, and to all enquiring Friends, and believe me ever

My dear Sister

Your affectionate Brother

B. Franklin

PATER FAMILIAS

LONDON agent of several American colonies, Fellow of the Royal Society, center of an admiring circle of friends, Franklin was nonetheless head of a Philadelphia family. English politics and the new science were never so engrossing that he could not discuss household matters with Deborah, his wife and "dear child" in far-away America. At her order he purchased London finery; with her he exchanged views on painting the house and arranging the furniture; he soberly considered the terms of his daughter Sally's prospective marriage to the young merchant Richard Bache and advised how it should be conducted; and, though he moved in a great world, he listened to Deborah's news and gossip and planned for the time he would return to Market Street to pass a pleasant evening at her side.

To Deborah Franklin

London, June 22, 1767

My dear Child,

Capt. Falkener is arriv'd, and came yesterday to see me, and bring my Letters. I was extreamly glad of yours, because I had none by the Packet.

17

It seems now as if I should stay here another Winter, and therefore I must leave it to your Judgment to act in the Affair of your Daughter's Match as shall seem best. If you think it a suitable one, I suppose the sooner it is compleated, the better. In that case, I would only advise that you do not make an expensive feasting Wedding, but conduct every thing with Frugality and Economy, which our Circumstances really now require to be observed in all our Expences; For since my Partnership with Mr. Hall is expired, a great Source of our Income is cut off; and if I should lose the Post Office, which among the many Changes here is far from being unlikely, we should be reduc'd to our Rents and Interest of Money for a Subsistence, which will by no means afford the chargeable Housekeeping and Entertainments we have been used to;—for my own Part I live here as frugally as possible not to be destitute of the Comforts of Life, making no Dinners for any body, and contenting my self with a single Dish when I dine at home; and yet such is the Dearness of Living here in every Article, that my Expences amaze me. I see too by the Sums you have received in my Absence, that yours are very great, and I am very sensible that your Situation naturally brings you a great many Visitors which occasion an Expence not easily to be avoided, especially when one has been long in the Practice and Habit of it: But when People's Incomes are lessened if they cannot proportionably lessen their Outgoings, they must come to Poverty. If we were young enough to begin Business again, it might be another Matter, but I doubt we are past it; and Business not well managed ruins one faster than no Business. In short, with Frugality and prudent Care we may subsist decently on what we have, and leave it entire to our Children: but without such Care, we shall not be able to keep it together; it will melt away like Butter in the Sunshine; and we may live long enough to feel the miserable Consequences of our Indiscretion.

I know very little of the Gentleman or his Character, nor can I at this Distance. I hope his Expectations are not great of any Fortune to be had with our Daughter before our Death. I can only say: that if he proves a good

18

DEBORAH FRANKLIN
Oil painting by Matthew Pratt

Husband to her, and a good Son to me, he shall find me as good a Father as I can be: but at present I suppose you would agree with me that we cannot do more than fit her out handsomely in Cloaths and Furniture, not exceeding in the whole Five Hundred Pounds, of Value. For the rest, they must depend as you and I did, on their own Industry and Care: as what remains in our Hands will be barely sufficient for our Support, and not enough for them when it comes to be divided at our Decease.

Having lately bought a Piece of fine Pocket Handkerchiefs, I send you 4 of them, being Half the Piece; and shall look out for the Quilts you mention, that is, Mrs. Stevenson will, and for the Muff and Snail for Sally.— None of the Things are yet come on shore.

I send you the little Shade that was copied from that great one. If it will be acceptable to my good Friend Mr. Roberts, pray give it to him.

Our Polly's Match is quite broke off. The Difference was about Money Matters. I am not displeas'd at it, as I did not much like the Man, thinking him a mean-spirited mercenary Fellow, and not worthy so valuable a Girl as she is in every Respect, Person, Fortune, Temper, and excellent Understanding.

Sally Franklin [an English relative] is well; her Father who had not seen her for a twelve month, came lately and took her home with him for a few Weeks to see her Friends: he is very desirous I should take her with me to America.

I suppose the blue Room is too blue, the Wood being of the same Colour with the Paper, and so looks too dark. I would have you finish it as soon as you can, thus. Paint the Wainscot a dead white; Paper the Walls blue, and tack the gilt Border round just above the Surbase and under the Cornish. If the Paper is not equal Coloured when pasted on, let it be brush'd over again with the same Colour: and let the Papier machée musical Figures be tack'd to the middle of the Cieling; when this is done, I think it will look very well.

Who is the Mrs. Morris you mention, as Mother to Dr. Rush? I am glad my Recommendations were of any Service to him.

I am glad to hear that Sally keeps up and increases the Number of her Friends. The best Wishes of a fond Father for her Happiness always attend her. I am, my dear Debby,   Your affectionate Husband

                                                        B. Franklin

A PEN HAS A SHARP POINT

FRIENDLINESS and warmth were characteristics of most of Franklin's personal letters, yet he could wield his pen in a very different manner when the occasion required. Jeremiah Meyer, a German artist residing in London, had promised to paint a miniature from a portrait which the Pennsylvania agent had placed in his hands. When this promise remained too long unfulfilled Franklin became annoyed, very much annoyed indeed. A brief and formal note conveyed to the artist his patron's displeasure.

To Jeremiah Meyer

[London, April 1771?]

Dr. Franklin presents his Compliments to Mr. Meyer, and prays him not to detain any longer the Picture from which he was to make a Miniature, but return it by the Bearer. Hopes Mr. Meyer will not think him impatient, as he has waited full Five Years, and seen many of his Acquaintance tho' applying later, serv'd before him. Wishes Mr. Meyer not to give himself the Trouble of making any more Apologies or to feel the least Pain on Account of his disappointing Dr. Franklin who assures him, he never was disappointed by him but once, not having for several Years past since he has known the Character of his Veracity, had the smallest dependance upon it.

THE sharp tone of Franklin's letter to the dilatory Jeremiah Meyer is in marked contrast to the cordiality of his attitude toward most artists and their work. Charles Willson Peale, a native of Maryland, first met Franklin in 1767 in London, where the young man had gone to study painting. The Pennsylvania agent befriended him and, back in America four years later, the artist wrote to tell of his progress as a portrait painter in Maryland and Philadelphia. The very practical Franklin replied to the thirty-year-old Peale with sound advice on the conduct of his affairs and with encouraging remarks on the future of the arts in America.

To Charles Willson Peale

London, July 4, 1771

Sir,

I received your obliging Letter of April 21 and it gave me great Pleasure to hear that you had met with such Encouragement at Philadelphia, and that you succeed so well in your Business in your native Country. If I were to advise you, it should be, by great Industry and Frugality to secure a Competency as early in Life as may be: For as your Profession requires good Eyes, cannot so well be follow'd with Spectacles, and therefore will not probably afford Subsistence *so long* as some other Employments, you have a Right to claim proportionably larger Rewards while you continue able to exercise it to general Satisfaction.

The Arts have always travelled Westward, and there is no doubt of their flourishing hereafter on our side the Atlantic, as the Number of wealthy Inhabitants shall increase, who may be able and willing suitably to reward them, since from several Instances it appears that our People are not deficient in Genius.

You have my best Wishes for your Prosperity and Happiness, being with great Regard, Sir   Your faithful humble
Servant
B. Franklin

—————

CONVERSATION IN A COACH

DURING the summer of 1771 Franklin spent three happy weeks at Twyford, near Winchester, England, at the home of his good friend Jonathan Shipley, Bishop of St. Asaph. In addition to one son, who was absent at the time, the family of the bishop and Mrs. Shipley consisted of five daughters ranging in age from Anna Maria, twenty-three, to Catherine Louisa ("Kitty"), about eleven. In these pleasant surroundings Franklin found inspiration to write the first long installment of his autobiography, in which he undertook to review the experiences of his sixty-five years of life and to draw from them such lessons as might be both interesting and useful to another generation. When the visit ended the Shipleys asked of him the favor of escorting their youngest daughter Kitty back to London, where she was to attend school.

How the elderly American, prominent on the political stage and world renowned as a scientist, and the eleven-year-old girl got on together in their day-long carriage journey was the subject of a prompt and detailed letter to his recent hostess. Nothing in all Franklin's writings better reveals why he was always such a favorite with young people. (In printing this letter quotation marks, not included in the original, have been added for the sake of clarity.)

To Mrs. Jonathan Shipley

London, August 12, 1771

Dear Madam,

This is just to let you know that we arriv'd safe and well in Marlborough Street about Six, where I deliver'd up my Charge:

22

The above seems too short for a Letter; so I will lengthen it by a little Account of our Journey. The first Stage we were rather pensive. I tried several Topics of Conversation, but none of them would hold. But after Breakfast we began to recover Spirits, and had a good deal of Chat. Will you hear some of it? We talk'd of her Brother, and she wish'd he was married. "And don't you wish your Sisters married too?" "Yes. All but Emily; I would not have her married." "Why?" "Because I can't spare her, I can't part with her. The rest may marry as soon as they please, so they do but get good Husbands." We then took upon us to consider for 'em what sort of Husbands would be fittest for every one of them. We began with Georgiana. She thought a Country Gentleman, that lov'd Travelling and would take her with him, that lov'd Books and would hear her read to him; I added "that had a good Estate and was a Member of Parliament and lov'd to see an Experiment now and then." This she agreed to; so we set him down for Georgiana, and went on to Betsy. "Betsy," says I, "seems of a sweet mild Temper, and if we should give her a Country Squire, and he should happen to be of a rough, passionate Turn, and be angry now and then, it might break her Heart." "O, none of 'em must be so; for then they would not be good Husbands." "To make sure of this Point, however, for Betsey, shall we give her a Bishop?" "O, no, that won't do. They all declare against the Church, and against the Army; not one of them will marry either a Clergyman or an Officer; that they are resolved upon." "What can be their reason for that?" "Why you know, that when a Clergyman or an Officer dies, the Income goes with 'em; and then what is there to maintain the Family? There's the Point." "Then suppose we give her a good, honest, sensible City Merchant, who will love her dearly and is very rich?" "I don't know but that may do." We proceeded to Emily, her dear Emily, I was afraid we should hardly find any thing good enough for Emily; but at last, after first settling that, if she did marry, Kitty was to live a good deal with her; we agreed that as Emily was very handsome we might expect an Earl for her. So

23

having fix'd her, as I thought, a Countess, we went on to Anna-Maria. "She," says Kitty, "should have a rich Man that has a large Family and a great many things to take care of; for she is very good at managing, helps my Mama very much, can look over Bills, and order all sorts of Family Business." "Very well; and as there is a Grace and Dignity in her Manner that would become the Station, what do you think of giving her a Duke?" "O no! I'll have the Duke for Emily. You may give the Earl to Anna-Maria if you please: But Emily shall have the Duke." I contested this Matter some time; but at length was forc'd to give up the point, leave Emily in Possession of the Duke, and content myself with the Earl for Anna Maria. "And now what shall we do for Kitty? We have forgot her, all this Time." "Well, and what will you do for her?" "I suppose that tho' the rest have resolv'd against the Army, she may not yet have made so rash a Resolution." "Yes, but she has: Unless, now, an old one, an old General that has done fighting, and is rich, such a one as General Rufane; I like him a good deal; You must know I like an old Man, indeed I do: And some how or other all the old Men take to me, all that come to our House like me better than my other Sisters: I go to 'em and ask 'em how they do, and they like it mightily; and the Maids take notice of it, and say when they see an old Man come, 'there's a Friend of yours, Miss Kitty.'" "But then as you like an old General, hadn't you better take him while he's a young Officer, and let him grow old upon your Hands, because then, you'll like him better and better every Year as he grows older and older." "No, that won't do. He must be an old Man of 70 or 80, and take me when I am about 30: And then you know I may be a rich young Widow." We din'd at Staines, she was Mrs. Shipley, cut up the Chicken pretty handily (with a little Direction) and help'd me in a very womanly Manner. "Now," says she, when I commended her, "my Father never likes to see me or Georgiana carve, because we do it, he says, badly: But how should we learn if we never try?" We drank good Papa and Mama's Health, and the Healths of the Dutchess, the Countess, the Merchant's Lady, the

24

Country Gentlewoman, and our Welsh Brother. This brought their Affairs again under Consideration. "I doubt," says she, "we have not done right for Betsey. I don't think a Merchant will do for her. She is much inclin'd to be a fine Gentlewoman; and is indeed already more of the fine Gentlewoman, I think, than any of my other Sisters; and therefore she shall be a Vice Countess."

Thus we chatted on, and she was very entertaining quite to Town.

I have now made my Letter as much too long as it was at first too short. The Bishop would think it too trifling, therefore don't show it him. I am afraid too that you will think it so, and have a good mind not to send it. Only it tells you Kitty is well at School, and for that I let it go. My Love to the whole amiable Family, best Respects to the Bishop, and 1000 Thanks for all your Kindnesses, and for the happy Days I enjoy'd at Twyford. With the greatest Esteem and Respect, I am,

Madam,

Your most obedient and humble Servant
B. Franklin

[*Editors' Postscript:* Catherine Louisa Shipley died in her eighty-second year—unmarried.]

———

PRUDENTIAL ALGEBRA

Friends and acquaintances as well as relations sought Franklin's counsel in their perplexities; and the courses he advised were moderate, just, and wise. In at least one case, however, he was willing to reveal to the anxious inquirer, a distinguished theologian and scientist, only *how* he might arrive at the decision himself. In its careful weighing of pros and cons the method was typical of Franklin; and typical of him and his age was its assumption of the rationality of men. Yet for all this, Franklin was a warmly appealing human being; no man was ever less a machine; and it would be preposterous to believe that Franklin loved his family, experimented with electricity, wrote the bagatelles, and signed the Declaration of Independence because the solution of an algebraic equation left him no alternative.

To Joseph Priestley

London, September 19, 1772

Dear Sir,

In the Affair of so much Importance to you, wherein you ask my Advice, I cannot for want of sufficient Premises, advise you *what* to determine, but if you please I will tell you *how*. When these difficult Cases occur, they are difficult chiefly because while we have them under Consideration all the Reasons *pro* and *con* are not present to the Mind at the same time; but sometimes one Set present themselves, and at other times another, the first being out of Sight. Hence the various Purposes or Inclinations that alternately prevail, and the Uncertainty that perplexes us. To get over this, my Way is, to divide half a Sheet of Paper by a Line into two Columns, writing over the one *Pro*, and over the other *Con*. Then during three or four Days Consideration I put down under the different Heads short Hints of the different Motives that at different Times occur to me for or against the Measure. When I have thus got them all together in one View, I endeavour to estimate their respective Weights; and where I find two, one on each side, that seem equal, I strike them both out: If I find a Reason *pro* equal to some two Reasons *con*, I strike out the three. If I judge some two Reasons *con* equal to some three Reasons *pro*, I strike out the five; and thus proceeding I find at length where the Ballance lies; and if after a Day or two of farther Consideration nothing new that is of Importance occurs on either side, I come to a Determination accordingly. And tho' the Weight of Reasons cannot be taken with the Precision of Algebraic Quantities, yet when each is thus considered separately and comparatively, and the whole lies before me, I think I can judge better, and am less likely to take a rash Step; and in fact I have

THE PHILOSOPHER AND COLONIAL AGENT
Oil painting by David Martin, 1767

found great Advantage from this kind of Equation, in what may be called *Moral* or *Prudential Algebra*. Wishing sincerely that you may determine for the best, I am ever, my dear Friend,

Yours most affectionately
B. Franklin

A NEW USE FOR MADEIRA WINE

CURRENT speculations on spontaneous generation and suspended animation intrigued Franklin. In response to a letter from his French friend Barbeu Dubourg he communicated observations and experiments he had made in a specific case of flies reviving after long immersion in wine. Then, concluding in mingled hopefulness and whimsy, he proposed a method by which, should it ever prove practicable, men might readily and comfortably enjoy an experience like Rip Van Winkle's.

To Jacques Barbeu Dubourg

[London, April 1773]

Your observations on the causes of death, and the experiments which you propose for recalling to life those who appear to be killed by lightning, demonstrate equally your sagacity and your humanity. It appears that the doctrine of life and death in general is yet but little understood.

A toad buried in sand may live, it is said, until the sand becomes petrified; and then, being inclosed in the stone, it may still live for we know not how many centuries. The facts which are cited in support of this opinion are too numerous, and too circumstantial not to deserve a certain degree of credit. As we are accustomed to see all living beings eat and drink, it appears to us difficult to conceive how a toad can be supported in such a dungeon. But if we reflect, that the necessity of nourishment of animals, in their ordinary state, proceeds from the continual waste of their substance by perspiration;

it will appear less incredible that some animals in a torpid state, perspiring less because they use no exercise, should have less need of aliment; and that others, which are covered with scales or shells, which stop perspiration, such as turtles, serpents, and some species of fish, should be able to subsist a considerable time without any nourishment whatever. A plant, with its flowers, soon fades and dies if exposed to the air, without having its roots immersed in a humid soil, from which it may draw a sufficient quantity of moisture to supply that which exhales from its substance, and is carried off continually by the air. Perhaps, however, if it were buried in quicksilver, it might preserve for a considerable space of time its vegetable life, its smell and colour. If this be the case, it might prove a good method of transporting from distant countries those delicate plants, which are unable to sustain the sea air and which require particular care and attention.

I have seen an instance of common flies preserved in a manner somewhat similar. They had been drowned in Madeira wine, apparently about the time when it was bottled in Virginia, to be sent here (to London). At the opening of one of the bottles, at the house of a friend where I was, three drowned flies fell into the first glass that was filled. Having heard it remarked that drowned flies came back to life in the sun, I proposed making the experiment upon these. They were therefore exposed to the sun upon a sieve which had been employed to strain them out of the wine. In less than three hours, two of them began by degrees to recover life. They commenced by some convulsive motions in the thighs, and at length they raised themselves upon their legs, wiped their eyes with their fore feet, beat and brushed their wings with their hind feet, and soon after flew away, finding themselves in Old England, without knowing how they came thither. The third continued lifeless till sun-set, when, losing all hopes of him, he was thrown away.

I wish it were possible, from this instance, to invent a method of embalming drowned persons, in such a manner that they might be recalled to

28

life at any period, however distant; for having a very ardent desire to see and observe the state of America an hundred years hence, I should prefer to an ordinary death, the being immersed with a few friends in a cask of Madeira, until that time, then to be recalled to life by the solar warmth of my dear country! But since, in all probability, we live in a century too little advanced, and too near the infancy of science, to see such an art brought in our time to its perfection, I must, for the present, content myself with the treat, which you are so kind as to promise me, of the resurrection of a fowl or a turkey cock.   I am, etc.

                                                        B. Franklin

----

A REVOLT BEGINS

UNTIL he was almost seventy years old Franklin was a loyal subject of the King and a firm believer in the mutual benefits both mother country and American colonies derived from the imperial union. During the last years of his residence in England as colonial agent he recognized with increasing clarity that the policies of extremists on both sides were undermining that union. In every possible way he could he urged upon the British a more enlightened course of action, but in vain. "Passion governs," he wrote an American friend, "and she never governs wisely." As to himself, "Anxiety begins to disturb my rest, and whatever robs an old Man of his Sleep, soon demolishes him." But he was, indeed, far from demolished. Upon reaching Philadelphia early in May 1775 he was greeted with the news of Lexington and Concord. He was old enough to be able to claim the right to retire, but there was no question in his mind of the course he should pursue. He plunged with characteristic energy into public business. Two months later he found time to write a long letter to his old friend Bishop Shipley. From the position he had now taken Franklin never wavered through more than eight years of war, until at last he had the satisfaction of signing the definitive treaty of peace between the new nation and his former sovereign.

To Jonathan Shipley

Philadelphia, July 7, 1775

I received with great Pleasure my dear Friend's very kind Letter of April 19, as it informed me of his Welfare, and that of the amiable Family in Jermyn Street. I am much obliged by the Information of what pass'd in Parliament after my departure; in return I will endeavor to give you a short Sketch of the State of Affairs here.

I found at my arrival all America from one End of the 12 united Provinces to the other, busily employed in learning the Use of Arms. The Attack upon the Country People near Boston by the Army had rous'd every Body and exasperated the whole Continent; The Tradesmen of this City were in the Field twice a day, at 5 in the Morning, and Six in the Afternoon, disciplining with the utmost Diligence, all being Volunteers. We have now three Battalions, a Troop of Light Horse, and a Company of Artillery who have made surprizing Progress. The same Spirit appears everywhere and the Unanimity is amazing.

The day after my Arrival, I was unanimously chosen by our Assembly, then sitting, an additional Delegate to the Congress, which met the next Week. The numerous Visits of old Friends, and the publick Business has since devoured all my time: for We meet at nine in the Morning, and often sit 'till four. I am also upon a Committee of Safety appointed by the Assembly, which meets at Six, and sits 'till near nine. The Members attend closely without being bribed to it, by either Salary, Place or Pension, or the hopes of any; which I mention for your Reflection on the difference, between a new virtuous People, who have publick Spirit, and an old corrupt one, who have not so much as an Idea that such a thing exists in

Nature. There has not been a dissenting Voice among us in any Resolution for Defence, and our Army which is already formed, will soon consist of above 20,000 Men.

You will have heard before this reaches you of the Defeat the Ministerial Troops met with on their first *Sortie;* the several small Advantages we have since had of them, and the more considerable Affair of the 17th when after two severe Repulses, they carry'd the unfinished Trenches of the Post we had just taken on a Hill near Charlestown. They suffered greatly however, and I believe are convinc'd by this time, that they have Men to deal with, tho' unexperienced, and not yet well arm'd. In their way to this Action, without the least Necessity, they barbarously plundered and burnt a fine, undefended Town, opposite to Boston, called Charlestown, consisting of about 400 Houses, many of them elegantly built; some sick, aged and decrepit poor Persons, who could not be carried off in time perish'd in the Flames. In all our Wars, from our first settlement in America, to the present time, we never received so much damage from the Indian *Savages,* as in this one day from these. Perhaps Ministers may think this a Means of disposing us to Reconciliation. I feel and see every where the Reverse. Most of the little Property I have, consists of Houses in the Seaport Towns, which I suppose may all soon be destroyed in the same way, and yet I think I am not half so reconcileable now, as I was a Month ago.

The Congress will send one more Petition to the King, which I suppose will be treated as the former was, and therefore will probably be the last; for tho' this may afford Britain one chance more of recovering our Affections and retaining the Connection, I think she has neither Temper nor Wisdom enough to seize the Golden Opportunity. When I look forward to the Consequences, I see an End to all Commerce between us: on our Sea Coasts She may hold some fortified Places as the Spaniards do on the Coast of Africa, but can penetrate as little into the Country: a very numerous Fleet extending 1500 Miles at an immense Expense may prevent other

Nations trading with us: but as we have or may have within ourselves every thing necessary to the Comfort of Life, and generally import only Luxuries and Superfluities, her preventing our doing that, will in some Respects contribute to our Prosperity. By the present Stoppage of our Trade we save between four and five Millions per Ann which will do something towards the Expence of the War. What *she* will get by it, I must leave to be computed by her own political Arithmeticians. These are some of my present Ideas which I throw out to you in the Freedom of Friendship. Perhaps I am too sanguine in my opinion of our Abilities for the Defence of our Country after we shall have given up our Seaports to Destruction, but a little time will shew.

General Gage we understand enter'd into a Treaty with the Inhabitants of Boston, whom he had confin'd by his Works, in which Treaty it was agreed that if they delivered their Arms to the Select Men, their own Magistrates, they were to be permitted to go out with their *Effects*. As soon as they had so delivered their Arms, he seiz'd them, and then cavil'd about the meaning of the word *Effects* which he said was only wearing Apparel and Household Furniture, and not Merchandize or Shop Goods, which he therefore detains; and the continual Injuries and Insults they met with from the Soldiery, made them glad to get out by relinquishing all that kind of Property. How much those People have suffered, and are now suffering rather than submit to what they think unconstitutional Acts of Parliament is really amazing. Two or three Letters I send you enclosed may give you some, tho' a faint Idea of it. Gage's Perfidy has now made him universally detested. When I consider that all this Mischief is done my Country, by Englishmen and Protestant Christians, of a Nation among whom I have so many personal Friends, I am ashamed to feel any Consolation in a prospect of Revenge; I chuse to draw it rather from a Confidence that we shall sooner or later obtain Reparation. I have proposed therefore to our People that they keep just Accounts, and never resume the Commerce or the

Union, 'till Satisfaction is made. If it is refused for 20 Years, I think we shall then be able to take it with Interest.

Your excellent Advice was, that if we must have a War, let it be carried on as between Nations who had once been Friends, and wish to be so again. In this ministerial War against us, all Europe is conjur'd not to sell us Arms or Amunition, that we may be found defenceless, and more easily murdered. The humane Sir W. Draper, who had been hospitably entertain'd in every one of our Colonies, proposes, in his Papers call'd the Traveller, to excite the Domestic Slaves, you have sold us, to cut their Master's Throats. Dr. Johnson a Court Pensioner, in his *Taxation no Tyranny* adopts and recommends that Measure, together with another of hiring the Indian Savages to assassinate our Planters in the Back-Settlements. They are the poorest and most innocent of all People, and the Indian manner is to murder and scalp Men Women and Children. This Book I heard applauded by Lord Sandwich in Parliament, and all the ministerial People recommended it. Lord Dunmore and Governor Martin, have already, we are told, taken some Steps towards carrying one part of the Project into Execution, by exciting an Insurrection among the Blacks. And Governor Carleton, we have certain Accounts, has been very industrious in engaging the Indians to begin their horrid Work. This is making War like Nations who never had been Friends, and never wish to be such while the World stands. You see I am warm: and if a Temper naturally cool and phlegmatic can, in old age, which often cools the warmest, be thus heated, you will judge by that of the general Temper here, which is now little short of Madness. We have however as yet ask'd no foreign Power to assist us, nor made any offer of our Commerce to other Nations for their Friendship. What another year's Persecution may drive us to, is yet uncertain. I drop this disagreeable Subject, and will take up one, that I know must afford you and the good Family, as my Friends, some Pleasure. It is the State of my own Family, which I found in good Health; my Children affection-

33

ately dutifull and attentive to every thing that can be agreeable to me; with three very promising Grandsons, in whom I take great Delight So that were it not for our Publick Troubles, and the being absent from so many that I love in England, my present Felicity would be as perfect, as in this World one could well expect it. I enjoy however, what there is of it while it lasts, mindfull at the same time that its Continuance is like other earthly Goods, uncertain. Adieu my dear Friend, and believe me ever, with sincere and great Esteem

Yours most Affectionately

B. Franklin

My respectfull Complts. to Mrs. Shipley.

Your Health on this side the Water is every where drank by the Name of THE Bishop.

I send for your Amusement a Parcel of our Newspapers. When you have perused them, please to give them to Mr. Hartley of Golden Square.

―――

HOW TO PAY FOR A WAR

IN the autumn of 1775 Congress appointed Franklin one of a committee of three to go to Washington's headquarters at Cambridge, Massachusetts, to confer with the Commander-in-chief on the problem of supporting and regulating the Continental Army. From Cambridge he wrote back to his son-in-law Richard Bache in Philadelphia. On his return home, Franklin explained, he would call for his sister Jane Mecom, who had fled from Boston to friends in Rhode Island at the beginning of the siege. Then, turning to the subject of war, Franklin commented on the spirit of the people at Boston, and, in characteristic fashion, worked out arithmetically a way to finance its costs.

34

To Richard Bache

Dear Son

We hear you have had an Alarm at Philadelphia. I hope no ill consequences have attended it. I wonder I had no Line from you. I make no
doubt of our People's defending their City and Country bravely, on the
most trying Occasions.

I hear nothing yet of Mr. Goddard, but suppose he is on the Road. I
suppose we shall leave this Place next Week. I shall not return in Company
with the other Delegates, as I must call for my Sister, and we shall hardly
be able to travel so fast, but I expect to be at Philadelphia within a few
Days of them.

There has been a plentiful Year here as well as with us: And there are as
many chearful Countenances among those who are driven from House and
Home at Boston or lost their All at Charlestown, as among other Peoples.
Not a Murmur has yet been heard, that if they had been less zealous in the
Cause of Liberty they might still have enjoy'd their Possessions. For my
own Part tho' I am for the most prudent Parsimony of the publick Treasure, I am not terrified by the Expence of this War, should it continue ever
so long. A little more Frugality, or a little more Industry in Individuals will
with Ease defray it. Suppose it 100,000£ a month or 1,200,000£ a Year:
If 500,000 Families will each spend a Shilling a Week less, or earn a Shilling
a Week more; or if they will spend 6 pence a Week less and earn 6 pence
a Week more, they may pay the Whole Sum without otherwise feeling it.
Forbearing to drink Tea saves three fourths of the Money; and 500,000
Women doing each threepence Worth of Spinning or Knitting in a Week
will pay the rest.* I wish nevertheless most earnestly for Peace, this War

35

being a truly unnatural and mischievous one: but we have nothing to expect from Submission but Slavery, and Contempt. I am ever

Your affectionate Father

Love to dear Sally and the   B. F[ranklin]
    Children.

       *How much more then may be done by the superior
       Frugality and Industry of the Men?

━━━━━

A SCIENTIST TURNS POLITICIAN

JAN INGENHOUSZ, a Dutch-born doctor of medicine and physicist, lived for some years in England before he became body physician to the Emperor of Austria at Vienna in 1769. During his English residence he and Franklin, both interested in scientific matters, struck up a friendship which they continued by correspondence almost to the end of Franklin's life. Most of their letters dealt with topics in the field of "philosophy," as science was then generally called, and even during the Revolution Ingenhousz kept Franklin posted on the latest developments which came to his attention in Vienna. Franklin, of course, was much too busy to indulge his own love for scientific experimentation during his years as minister to France, where he arrived late in 1776, but he welcomed his friend's letters and wrote back when he could. The letter here printed, written in two installments, is partly a reporting of personal and family news and partly a mixture of political discussion and scientific comment. In reading between the lines it is easy to recognize the hope of the aging American "philosopher"—now seventy-one—that a speedy and successful end to the war might yet enable him to return to his dearest love, the pursuit of scientific study and experimentation.

36

To Jan Ingenhousz

My dear Friend,

I received your kind Letter of the 4th of January. It gave me great Pleasure, as it inform'd me of your Welfare, and of the Continuance of your Friendship, which I highly value. If his Imperial Majesty's Journey to France is only postponed, and not entirely laid aside, I hope I may still have the Happiness of seeing you, as I suppose it will not be so inconvenient to you to travel hither in his Suite, as it would be to go to England (as you wish to do) alone.

Mr. Collard has not sent me the Letter you mention, so that I know not the Contents of it, otherwise I should now answer it. I have waited already too long in Expectation of it.

I long laboured in England with great Zeal, and Sincerity to prevent the Breach that has happened, and which is now so wide that no Endeavours of mine can possibly heal it. You know the Treatment I met with from that imprudent Court: But I keep a separate Account of private Injuries, which I may forgive; and I do not think it right to mix them with publick Affairs. Indeed there is no Occasion for their Aid to sharpen my Resentment against a Nation, that has burnt our defenceless Towns in the midst of Winter, has excited the Savages to assassinate our innocent Farmers with their Wives and Children, and our Slaves to murder their Masters. It would therefore be deceiving you, if I suffer'd you to remain in the Supposition you have taken up, that I am come hither to make Peace. I am in fact ordered hither by the Congress for a very different Purpose, viz. to procure such Aids from European Powers for enabling us to defend our Freedom and Independence, as it is certainly their Interest to grant, as by that means the great and rapidly growing Trade of America will be open to them all, and not a Monopoly to Britain as heretofore; a Monopoly, that if she is suffer'd again to possess, will be such an Increase of her Strength by Sea, and if she can reduce us again to Submission, she will have thereby so great an Addition to her Strength by Sea and Land, as will together make her the most formidable Power the World has yet seen, and, from her natural Pride and Insolence in Prosperity, of all others the most intolerable.

You will excuse my writing Politicks to you, as your Letter has given me the Occasion. Much more pleasing would it be to me to discuss with you some Point of Philosophy: And I am ready to promise you, that whenever you give me an Opportunity of enjoying that Pleasure in your Company, you shall not hear a Word from me on any other Subject, or against your Favourite Nation.

I have lately heard from our excellent Friend Sir John Pringle. He is well, except his *Insomnie*, which I fear grows upon him.

They tell me here that you are married. I congratulate you on that happy Change in your Situation. It is the most natural State of Man. I have lately lost my old and faithful Companion; and I every day become more sensible of the greatness of that Loss; which cannot now be repair'd. Present my respectful Compliments to your Spouse, and believe me ever, with sincere and great Esteem,

My dear Friend,

Yours most affectionately

B. Franklin

March 6, Passy near Paris

Just as I had finish'd writing the above, I receiv'd your Favour of January 29 with the other you had written to me in November last. Being exceedingly occupied here with Business, and moreover continually interrupted by the Civility of Visits, I have insensibly postpon'd to this time the Answer to those Letters, and have kept, unnecessarily, what I had written, to go with that Answer. Excuse, my dear Friend, this Delay. Old Men, I find are not so active as young ones.

With regard to securing Magazines of Gunpowder, I have seen no reason to vary from my Opinion since the Directions given for that at Purfleet. Possibly some Improvements may occur to you, when you are giving the Directions required of you, in which I wish you Success. There is a Paper of mine, in the French Edition, which contains some of the principal Arguments, Experiments and Facts, upon which the Practice is founded.

You desire to know my Opinion of what will probably be the End of this War? and whether our new Establishments will not be thereby reduced again to Deserts? I do not, for my part, apprehend much Danger of so great an Evil to us: I think, we shall be able; with a little Help, to defend ourselves, our Possessions and our Liberties, so long, that England will be ruined by persisting in the wicked Attempt to destroy them. I must nevertheless regret that Ruin, and wish that her Injustice and Tyranny had not deserv'd it. And I sometimes flatter myself, that, old as I am, I may possibly live to see my Country settled in Peace and Prosperity, when Britain shall make no more a formidable Figure among the Powers of Europe.

As to the present State of our Affairs, which you desire to be inform'd of, the English have long boasted much in their Gazettes of their Successes against us; but our latest Advices are, that they have been repuls'd in their intended Invasion of Pensylvania, and driven back thro' New Jersey to New York, with considerable Loss in three Engagements; so that the Campaign probably will end pretty much as it began; leaving them only in Possession of the Islands, which their naval Strength secures to them: and we shall in the next Campaign be much better provided with Arms, and Ammunition for their Entertainment on the Continent, where our Force is to consist of 84 Battalions.

You put me in mind of an Apology [*that is*, a justification] for my Conduct, which had been expected from me, in answer to the Abuses thrown upon me before the Privy Council. It was partly written; but the Affairs of public Importance I have been ever since engag'd in, prevented my finishing it. The injuries, too, that my Country has suffer'd, have absorb'd private Resentments, and made it appear trifling for an Individual to trouble the World with his particular Justification, when all his Compatriots were stigmatiz'd by the King and Parliament, as being in every respect the worst of Mankind. I am oblig'd to you, however, for the friendly Part you have always taken in the Defence of my Character; and it is indeed no small Argument in my favour, that those who have known me most and longest, still love me and trust me with their most important Interests, of which my Election into the Congress by the unanimous Voice of the Assembly or Parliament of Pennsylvania the Day after my Arrival from England, and my present Mission hither by the Congress itself, are Instances incontestible.

I thank you for the Account you give me of M. Volta's Experiment. You judge rightly in supposing that I have not much time at present to consider philosophical Matters: But as far as I understand it from your Description, it is only another Form of the Leiden Phial, and explicable by the same Principles. I must however own myself puzzled by one Part of your Account, viz. "and thus the electric Force once excited may be kept alive Years together"; which perhaps is only a Mistake. I have known it indeed to be continued many Months in a Phial hermetically sealed, and suppose it may be so preserved for Ages; But though one may by repeatedly touching the Knob of a charg'd Bottle with a small insulated Plate like the upper one of the Electrophore, draw successively an incredible Number of Sparks, that is, one after every Touch, and those for a while not apparently different in Magnitude, yet at length they will become small, and the Charge be finally exhausted. But I am in the wrong to give any Opinion till I have seen the Experiment.

I like much your Pasteboard Machine, and think it may in some respects be preferable to the very large Glass ones constructed here. The Duke de Chaulnes has one, said, if I remember right, to be 5 feet in Diameter. I saw it try'd, but it happen'd not to be in Order.

40

You inquire what is become of my Son, the Governor of New Jersey. As he adhered to the Party of the King, his People took him Prisoner, and sent him under a Guard to Connecticut, where he continues but is allow'd a District of some Miles to ride about, upon his Parole of Honour not to quit that Country. I have with me here his Son, a promising Youth of about 17, whom I brought with me, partly to finish his Education, having a great Affection for him, and partly to have his Assistance as a Clerk, in which Capacity he is very serviceable to me. I have also here with me my worthy Nephew, Mr. Williams, whom you kindly ask after. The ingenious Mr. Canton, our other Fellow Traveller, I suppose you know is now no more.

God bless you, my dear Friend, and believe me ever,

Yours most affectionately

B. Franklin

HOW TO RECOMMEND A STRANGER

IN France Franklin was almost swamped by Frenchmen and other Europeans seeking favors. Many of them wanted commissions in the American Army, though their only qualifications, other than some very slight military experience, seemed often to consist in having a large number of hungry children to support and a fervently expressed love of *la liberté*. Other applicants wanted letters of introduction to leading Americans because they planned to cross the Atlantic either just to see the country or to make their everlasting fortunes. Many were unknown to Franklin personally; some asked for recommendations for friends of theirs of whom he had never before heard. He knew that one of his main jobs in France was to act as an ambassador of good will, so he restrained his irritation at these importunities as best he could. One time, however, he relieved his feelings by composing a "Model of a Letter of Recommendation of a Person you are unacquainted with," which he could sign in perfect honesty without, perhaps, doing too much harm to Franco-American relations. There is no evidence that he ever gave this letter to an actual applicant, but at least the writing of it afforded him a little fun and some emotional relief.

To ————

Paris, April 2, 1777

Sir

The Bearer of this who is going to America, presses me to give him a Letter of Recommendation, tho' I know nothing of him, not even his Name. This may seem extraordinary, but I assure you it is not uncommon here. Sometimes indeed one unknown Person brings me another equally unknown, to recommend him; and sometimes they recommend one another! As to this Gentleman, I must refer you to himself for his Character and Merits, with which he is certainly better acquainted than I can possibly be. I recommend him however to those Civilities which every Stranger, of whom one knows no Harm, has a Right to, and I request you will do him all the good Offices and show him all the Favour that on further Acquaintance you shall find him to deserve. I have the honour to be, etc.

[B. Franklin]

TWELVE COMMANDMENTS

LIFE as American representative in France was demanding and often tedious; Franklin's official correspondence was heavy and usually rather dull. So he was the more grateful for the warm friendships he formed with several individuals in Paris, especially with women. Cheerfully and gracefully these ladies promoted his republican propaganda and assisted his diplomatic efforts; and in their company and in the letters he exchanged with some of them he discovered an agreeable relaxation. His personal letters

42

during these years, particularly those to two or three younger French women, are among the most sparkling he ever wrote. None make more entertaining reading than those he addressed to Madame Brillon, wife of a French official who also was a good friend of the American.

French society at that time permitted and even encouraged a much freer expression of gallantry and of intimacy between the sexes than American conventions, then or today, would allow; and Franklin, though in his seventies, accepted the challenge with delight. For this reason his letters to Madame Brillon have often been misunderstood; more has sometimes been read into them than he or she probably would have intended. The relation between the two was almost certainly platonic, however gaily and often he proposed that it be converted to another basis. She called him "my dear Papa," but insisted on remaining merely his friend and "confessor."

To Madame d'Hardancourt Brillon

Passy, March 10, 1778

I am charm'd with the Goodness of my Spiritual Guide, and resign myself implicitly to her Conduct, as she promises to lead me to Heaven in a Road so delicious, when I could be content to travel thither even in the roughest of all the Ways with the Pleasure of her Company.

How kindly partial to her Penitent, in finding him, on examining his Conscience, guilty of only one capital Sin, and to call that by the gentle Name of a *Foible!*

I lay fast hold of your Promise to absolve me of all Sins past, present, and *future*, on the easy and pleasing Condition of loving God, America, and my Guide above all things. I am in Raptures when I think of being absolv'd of the *future*.

People commonly speak of *Ten* Commandments. I have been taught that there are *twelve*. The *first* was, *Increase and multiply* and replenish the Earth. The *twelfth* is, A new Commandment I give unto you, *that ye love*

43

one another. It seems to me that they are a little misplac'd, and that the last should have been the first. However, I never made any Difficulty about that, but was always willing to obey them both whenever I had an Opportunity. Pray tell me, my dear Casuist, whether my keeping religiously these two Commandments, tho' not in the Decalogue, may not be accepted in Compensation for my breaking so often one of the Ten, I mean that which forbids Coveting my Neighbor's Wife, and which *I confess* I break constantly, God forgive me, as often as I see or think of my lovely Confessor: And I am afraid I should never be able to repent of the Sin, even if I had the full Possession of her.

And now I am consulting you upon a Case of Conscience, I will mention the Opinion of a certain Father of the Church, which I find myself willing to adopt, tho' I am not sure it is orthodox. It is this, That the most effectual Way to get rid of a certain Temptation, is, as often as it returns, to comply with and satisfy it. Pray instruct me how far I may venture to practise upon this Principle?

But why should I be so scrupulous, when you have promised to absolve me of the *future!*

Adieu, my charming Conductress, and believe me ever, with the sincerest Esteem and Affection,

Your most obedient and humble Servant

[B. Franklin]

FATHER IS NOT PLEASED

PERHAPS the heaviest sacrifice Franklin had to make for his country through service in France as American minister in France was separation from his family for nearly nine years. Many of his letters mention his longing to see his nearest relatives and his feeling of privation, in spite of his popularity in France. He had taken two grandsons with him to Europe. William Temple

Franklin (usually called "Temple"), whose father had been the last royal governor of New Jersey, was about nineteen in 1779 and was his grandfather's unofficial clerk at Passy, though some Americans were uneasy because a Tory's son occupied so confidential a position and were urging his removal. Benjamin Franklin Bache ("Ben" or "Benny") was only ten and at school, first near Paris, then in Geneva. Since Deborah Franklin had died late in 1774 and his son William was now completely estranged from his father, the old man counted as his closest of kin his sister Jane Mecom in Boston and his daughter Sarah Bache in Philadelphia. Sally was the delight of his heart, yet as a good father he had no hesitation in pointing out to her the error of her ways, when he deemed it necessary, even after she was a grown woman and several times a mother.

To Sarah Bache

Passy, June 3, 1779

Dear Sally,

I have before me your letters of October 22, and January 17th: they are the only ones I received from you in the course of eighteen months. If you knew how happy your letters make me, and considered how many miscarry, I think you would write oftener.

I am much obliged to the Miss Cliftons for the kind care they took of my house and furniture. Present my thankful acknowledgments to them, and tell them I wish them all sorts of happiness.

The clay medallion of me you say you gave to Mr. Hopkinson was the first of the kind made in France. A variety of others have been made since of different sizes; some to be set in lids of snuff boxes, and some so small as to be worn in rings; and the numbers sold are incredible. These, with the pictures, busts, and prints, (of which copies upon copies are spread every where) have made your father's face as well known as that of the moon, so that he durst not do any thing that would oblige him to run

45

away, as his phiz would discover him wherever he should venture to show it. It is said by learned etymologists that the name *Doll,* for the images children play with, is derived from the word IDOL; from the number of *dolls* now made of him, he may be truly said, *in that sense,* to be *i-doll-ized* in this country.

I think you did right to stay out of town till the summer was over for the sake of your child's health. I hope you will get out again this summer during the hot months; for I begin to love the dear little creature from your description of her.

I was charmed with the account you give me of your industry, the table-cloths of your own spinning, etc. but the latter part of the paragraph, that you had sent for linen from France because weaving and flax were grown dear; alas, that dissolved the charm; and your sending for long black pins, and lace, and *feathers!* disgusted me as much as if you had put salt into my strawberries. The spinning, I see, is laid aside, and you are to be dressed for the ball! you seem not to know, my dear daughter, that of all the dear things in this world, idleness is the dearest, except mischief.

The project you mention of removing Temple from me was an unkind one; to deprive an old man sent to serve his country in a foreign one, of the comfort of a child to attend him, to assist him in health and take care of him in sickness, would be cruel, if it was practicable. In this case it could not be done; for as the pretended suspicions of him are groundless, and his behaviour in every respect unexceptionable; I should not part with the child, but with the employment. But I am confident that whatever may be proposed by weak or malicious people, the Congress is too wise and too good to think of treating me in that manner.

Ben, if I should live long enough to want it, is like to be another comfort to me: as I intend him for a Presbyterian as well as a Republican, I have sent him to finish his education at Geneva. He is much grown, in very good health, draws a little, as you will see by the inclosed, learns Latin,

46

Drawn & Engraved by W.Birch & Son. Published by R.Campbell &C.N.º.30 Chesnut Street Philad.ª.1.º.1800.

PHILADELPHIA IN THE LATE EIGHTEENTH CENTURY

writing, arithmetic and dancing, and speaks French better than English. He made a translation of your last letter to him, so that some of your works may now appear in a foreign language. He has not been long from me. I send the accounts I have of him, and I shall put him in mind of writing to you. I cannot propose to you to part with your own dear Will: I must one of these days go back to see him; happy to be once more all together! but futurities are uncertain. Teach him however in the mean time to direct his worship more properly, for the deity of Hercules is now quite out of fashion.

The present you mention as sent by me, was rather that of a merchant at Bourdeaux, for he would never give me any account of it, and neither Temple nor I know any thing of the particulars.

When I began to [re]ad your account of the high prices of goods, "*a pair of gloves seven dollars, a yard of common gause twenty-four dollars, and that it now required a fortune to maintain a family in a very plain way,*" I expected you would conclude with telling me, that every body as well as yourself was grown frugal and industrious; and I could scarce believe my eyes in reading forward, that "*there never was so much dressing and pleasure going on;*" and that you yourself wanted *black pins and feathers from France,* to appear, I suppose, in the mode! This leads me to imagine that perhaps, it is not so much that the goods are grown dear, as that the money is grown cheap, as every thing else will do when excessively plenty; and that people are still as easy nearly in their circumstances as when a pair of gloves might be had for half a crown. The war indeed may in some degree raise the prices of goods, and the high taxes which are necessary to support the war may make our frugality necessary; and as I am always preaching that doctrine, I cannot in conscience or in decency encourage the contrary, by my example, in furnishing my children with foolish modes and luxuries. I therefore send all the articles you desire that are useful and necessary, and omit the rest; for as you say you should "*have great pride in wearing any thing I send, and showing it as your father's taste;*" I must avoid giving you an opportunity of doing that with either lace or feathers. If you wear your cambric ruffles as I do, and take care not to mend the holes, they will come in time to be lace; and feathers, my dear girl, may be had in America from every cock's tail.

If you happen again to see General Washington, assure him of my very great and sincere respect, and tell him that all the old Generals here amuse themselves in studying the accounts of his operations, and approve highly of his conduct.

Present my affectionate regards to all friends that enquire after me, particularly Mr. Duffield and family, and write oftener, my dear child, to

Your loving father,

B. Franklin

――――

MONEY TALKS

EDWARD BRIDGEN, London merchant and Fellow of the Royal Society, was, according to Franklin, "a particular Friend of mine and a zealous one of the American cause." In September 1779 he wrote Franklin offering to furnish the Americans with copper for small coins and even expressed willingness to have them stamped out in England, if necessary, despite the war, if Franklin would supply the designs. The author of *Poor Richard's Almanack*, always interested in the improvement of mankind, saw a chance here to use again, and even more effectively, a device for mass education inculcating "industry and frugality" which had been so popular and successful in his days as a young printer. And, as an alert and imaginative public official in time of war, he also saw an opportunity for useful political propaganda.

To Edward Bridgen

Passy, October 2, 1779

Dear Sir

I received your favour of the 17th past, and the 2 Samples of Copper are since come to hand. The Metal seems to be very good, and the Price reasonable, but I have not yet received the orders necessary to justify my making the purchase proposed. There has indeed been an Intention to strike Copper Coin that may not only be useful as small Change, but serve other purposes. Instead of repeating continually upon every Halfpenny the dull Story that everybody knows, and what it would have been no loss to mankind if no body had ever known, that Geo III is king of Great Britain france and Irland etc. to put one side some important proverbs of Salomon, some pious moral, prudential or Œconomical Precept, the frequent Inculcation of which by seeing it every time one receives a Piece of money might make an Impression upon the mind Especially of young persons and tend to regulate the Conduct; such as on some *the fear of the Lord is the Beginning of wisdom;* on others *honesty is the best Policy;* on others *he that by the Plow would thrive; himself must either lead or drive,* on others *keep thy Shop and thy Shop will keep thee;* on others *A Penny sav'd is a Penny got.* on others, *he that buys what he has no need of, will soon be forc'd to sell his necessaries.* on others, *Early to rise, will make a Man healthy wealthy and Wise.* and so on to a great variety. The other side it was propos'd to fill with good designs drawn and engrav'd by the Best artists in France of all the different Species of Barbarity with which the English have carry'd on the War in America expressing every abominable Circumstance of their Cruelty and inhumanity, that the figures can express, to make an Impression on the Minds of Posterity as Strong and durable as that on the Copper. This Resolution has been along time forborne, but the late Burning deffenceless Towns in Connecticut, on the flimsey Pretence that the People fired from behind their houses, when it is known

49

to have been premeditated and ordered from England, will probably give the finishing Provocation and may occasion a vast Demand for your Metal.

I thank you for your kind Wishes respecting my Health. I return them most cordially four fold into your own Bosome. Adieu.

[B. Franklin]

THE DELIGHTFUL LADIES OF FRANCE

FRANKLIN formed close personal friendships with several men and women in France and they gave him constant help in his work for the American cause. In a wider circle, too, he won great popularity. His homely manner so unlike theirs, his reasonableness so far from cynicism, his wit that had the freshness of clean earth, completely charmed the fashionable ladies of the Paris salons, and they, in turn, charmed him. The social conventions of the French capital differed sharply from those of Boston, yet his sisters and nieces in the New England community shared him willingly. "I Love, I almost Adore the French Ladies for their Kindness to you," his stepniece Elizabeth (Hubbard) Partridge exclaimed to him. This warm expression of love for those who loved him induced the seventy-three-year-old Franklin to explain more fully "that matter" of their extraordinary attentions.

To Elizabeth Partridge

Passy, October 11, 1779

Your kind Letter, my dear Friend, was long in coming; but it gave me the Pleasure of knowing that you had been well in October and January last. The Difficulty, Delay and Interruption of Correspondence with those I love, is one of the great Inconveniencies I find in living so far from home: but we must bear these and more, with Patience, if we can; if not, we must bear them as I do with Impatience.

50

You mention the Kindness of the French Ladies to me. I must explain that matter. This is the civilest Nation upon Earth. Your first Acquaintances endeavour to find out what you like, and they tell others. If 'tis understood that you like Mutton, dine where you will you find Mutton. Somebody, it seems, gave it out that I lov'd Ladies; and then every body presented me their Ladies (or the Ladies presented themselves) to be *embrac'd*, that is to have their Necks kiss'd. For as to kissing of Lips or Cheeks, it is not the Mode here: the first is reckon'd rude, and the other may rub off the Paint. The French Ladies have however 1000 other ways of rendering themselves agreeable; by their various Attentions and Civilities, and their sensible Conversation. 'Tis a delightful People to live with.

I thank you for the Boston Newspapers, tho' I see nothing so clearly in them as that your Printers do indeed want new Letters. They perfectly blind me in endeavouring to read them. If you should ever have any Secrets that you wish to be well kept, get them printed in those Papers. You enquire if Printers Types may be had here? Of all Sorts, very good, cheaper than in England, and of harder Metal. I will see any Orders executed in that way that any of your Friends may think fit to send. They will doubtless send Money with their Orders. Very good Printing Ink is likewise to be had here.

I cannot by this Opportunity send the Miniature you desire; but I send you a little Head in China, more like, perhaps, than the Painting would be. It may be set in a Locket, if you like it, cover'd with Glass, and may serve for the present. When Peace comes we may afford to be more extravagant. I send with it a Couple of Fatherly Kisses for you and your amiable Daughter, the whole wrapt up together in Cotton to be kept warm.

Present my respectful Compliments to Mr. Partridge.

Adieu, my dear Child, and believe me ever

Your affectionate Papah

[B. Franklin]

WITHOUT question the two most eminent Americans of the Revolutionary age were George Washington and Benjamin Franklin. Both were completely dedicated to a common cause and, although their personal contacts were few because Franklin was so long out of the country, each profoundly respected the other. Franklin's suggestion of a trip through Europe together after the war intrigues the imagination. Had it ever taken place it would certainly have produced a sensation wherever the famous planter-general and the equally famous scientist-diplomat went. Washington outlived Franklin by a little less than ten years. Before his death first signs had become visible of the promising future which the older man prophesied for the country they both had loved so much.

To George Washington

Passy, March 5, 1780

Sir,

I received but lately the Letter your Excellency did me the honour of writing to me in Recommendation of the Marquis de la Fayette. His Modesty detain'd it long in his own Hands. We became acquainted however, from the time of his Arrival at Paris, and his Zeal for the Honour of our Country, his Activity in our Affairs here, and his firm Attachment to our Cause, and to you, impress'd me with the same Regard and Esteem for him that your Excellency's Letter would have done, had it been immediately delivered to me.

Should Peace arrive after another Campaign or two, and afford us a little Leisure, I should be happy to see your Excellency in Europe, and to accompany you, if my Age and Strength would permit, in visiting some of its ancient and most famous Kingdoms. You would on this Side the Sea, enjoy the great Reputation you have acquir'd, pure and free from those little

Shades that the Jealousy and Envy of a Man's Countrymen and Contemporaries are ever endeavouring to cast over living Merit. Here you would know, and enjoy, what Posterity will say of Washington. For a 1000 Leagues have nearly the same Effect with 1000 Years. The feeble Voice of those groveling Passions cannot extend so far either in Time or Distance. At present I enjoy that Pleasure for you: as I frequently hear the old Generals of this martial Country, (who study the Maps of America, and mark upon them all your Operations) speak with sincere Approbation and great Applause of your Conduct, and join in giving you the Character of one of the greatest Captains of the Age.

I must soon quit the Scene, but you may live to see our Country flourish, as it will amazingly and rapidly after the War is over. Like a Field of young Indian Corn, which long Fair weather and Sunshine had enfeebled and discolour'd, and which in that weak State, by a Thunder Gust of violent Wind, Hail and Rain seem'd to be threatend with absolute Destruction; yet the Storm being once past, it recovers fresh Verdure, shoots up with double Vigour, and delights the Eye not of its Owner only, but of every observing Traveller.

The best Wishes that can be form'd, for your Health Honour and Happiness, ever attend you, from

Your Excellency's most obedient

and most humble Servant

B. F[ranklin]

—————

MISS VIRGINIA

TWICE in the course of the Revolution the Marquis de Lafayette received leave from Congress to make extended visits to his home in France. During these sojourns he and Franklin had considerable business to transact with one another and the two men became warm friends. On September 17, 1782, the young soldier proudly wrote the old statesman of the birth of a daughter, a seven-months' child. "They ask me what Name my daughter is to Have," he added. "I want to present her as an offering to My Western Country—And as there is a good Saint By the Name of Virginia, I was thinking if it would not be presuming too Much to let Her Bear a Name Similar to that of one of the United States." The same day Franklin wrote back, sending congratulations—and encouragement.

To the Marquis de Lafayette

Passy, September 17, 1782

Dear Sir

I continue to suffer from this cruel Gout: But in the midst of my Pain the News of Madame de la Fayette's safe Delivery, and your Acquisition of a Daughter gives me Pleasure.

In naming our Children I think you do well to begin with the most antient State. And as we cannot have too many of so good a Race, I hope you and Madame de la Fayette will go thro' the Thirteen. But as that may be in the common Way too severe a Task for her delicate Frame, and Children of Seven Months may become as Strong as those of Nine I consent to the Abridgement of Two Months for each; and I wish her to spend the Twenty-six Months so gained, in perfect Ease, Health and Pleasure.

While you are proceeding, I hope our States will some of them new-name themselves. Miss Virginia, Miss Carolina, and Miss Georgiana will sound prettily enough for the Girls; but Massachusetts and Connecticut, are too harsh even for the Boys, unless they were to be Savages.

That God may bless you in the Event of this Day as in every other, prays
Your affectionate Friend and Servant

B. Franklin

WHAT GOOD IS A NEW-BORN BABY?

THE War of the American Revolution had just come to a close when the French people, and Franklin with them, were offered a new interest and a fresh topic for speculation: human flight. After the Montgolfier brothers had several times sent aloft unmanned balloons inflated with hot air, two Frenchmen, Pilâtre de Rozier and the Marquis d'Arlandes, embarked in one of the Montgolfier craft, November 21, 1783, on what proved to be the first successful free-balloon flight of human beings in history, taking off from a spot near Franklin's house at Passy. Ten days later two other Frenchmen, Jacques Alexandre César Charles and one of the two Robert brothers, ascended from the Tuileries Gardens in Paris in a hydrogen-filled balloon. Franklin, a fascinated observer of both flights, reported these events to his scientific friends in other countries, especially to Sir Joseph Banks, the president of the Royal Society in London.

That the balloon was an astonishing toy many observers admitted, but of what possible good? What good, retorted Franklin in a reply that went the rounds of Paris, is a new-born baby? He was soon speculating on the effects of the new invention. In the second passage here, from a letter to Ingenhousz in Vienna a few weeks later, he proved, ironically, a better prophet of how air power might be used in war than of how it might contribute to universal peace.

To Sir Joseph Banks

Passy, December 1, 1783

Dear Sir,

In mine of yesterday, I promis'd to give you an Account of Messrs. Charles and Robert's Experiment, which was to have been made on this Day, and at which I intended to be present. Being a little indispos'd, and the Air cool, and the Ground damp, I declin'd going into the Garden of the Tuilleries where the Balloon was plac'd, not knowing how long I might be oblig'd to wait there before it was ready to depart; and chose to stay in my Carriage near the Statue of Louis XV. from whence I could well see it rise, and have an extensive View of the Region of Air thro' which, as the Wind sat, it was likely to pass. The Morning was foggy, but about One aClock, the Air became tolerably clear, to the great Satisfaction of the Spectators, who were infinite, Notice having been given of the intended Experiment several Days before in the Papers, so that all Paris was out, either about the Tuilleries, on the Quays and Bridges, in the Fields, the Streets, at the Windows, or on the Tops of Houses, besides the Inhabitants of all the Towns and Villages of the Environs. Never before was a philosophical Experiment so magnificently attended. Some Guns were fired to give Notice, that the Departure of the great Balloon was near, and a small one was discharg'd which went to an amazing Height, there being but little Wind to make it deviate from its perpendicular Course, and at length the Sight of it was lost. Means were used, I am told, to prevent the great Balloon's rising so high as might indanger its Bursting. Several Bags of Sand were taken on board before the Cord that held it down was cut; and the whole Weight being then too much to be lifted, such a Quantity was discharg'd as to permit its Rising slowly. Thus it would sooner arrive at that Region where it would be in Equilibrio with the surrounding Air, and by discharging more Sand afterwards, it might go higher if desired. Between One and Two aClock, all Eyes were gratified with seeing it rise majestically from among the Trees, and ascend gradually above the Buildings, a most beautiful Spectacle! When it was about 200 feet high, the brave Adventurers held out and wav'd a little white Pennant, on both sides their Carr, to salute the Spectators, who return'd loud Claps of Applause. The Wind was very little, so that the Object, tho' moving to the Northward, continued long in View; and it was a great while before the admiring People began to disperse. The Persons embark'd were Mr. Charles, Professor of Experimental Philosophy, and a zealous Promoter of that Science, and One of the Mes-

56

DESCENTE DE LA MACHINE
AEROSTATIQUE
Des S.rs Charles et Robert.

THE FIRST HYDROGEN BALLOON
The landing near L'Ile Adam

sieurs Robert, the very ingenious Constructors of the Machine. When it arriv'd at its height, which I suppose might be 3 or 400 Toises [1800 to 2400 feet], it appear'd to have only horisontal Motion. I had a Pocket Glass, with which I follow'd it, till I lost Sight, first of the Men, then of the Car, and when I last saw the Balloon, it appear'd no bigger than a Walnut. I write this at 7 in the Evening. What became of them is not yet known here. I hope they descended by Day-light, so as to see and avoid falling among Trees or on Houses, and that the Experiment was compleated without any mischievous Accident which the Novelty of it and the want of Experience might well occasion. I am the more anxious for the Event, because I am not well inform'd of the Means provided for letting themselves gently down, and the Loss of these very ingenious Men, would not only be a Discouragement to the Progress of the Art, but be a sensible Loss to Science and Society.

I shall inclose one of the Tickets of Admission, on which the Globe was represented, as originally intended, but is altered by the Pen to show its real State when it went off. When the Tickets were engraved, the Car was to have been hung to the Neck of the Globe, as represented by a little Drawing I have made in the Corner A. I suppose it may have been an Apprehension of Danger in straining too much the Balloon or tearing the Silk, that induc'd the Constructors to throw a Net over it, fix'd to a Hoop which went round its Middle, and to hang the Car to that Hoop, as you see in Fig. B.

Tuesday Morning, December 2. I am reliev'd from my Anxiety, by hearing that the Adventurers descended well near l'Isle Adam, before Sunset. This Place is near 7 Leagues from Paris. Had the Wind blown fresh, they might have gone much farther.

If I receive any farther Particulars of Importance, I shall communicate them hereafter.

With great Esteem, I am, dear Sir,

Your most obedient

and most humble Servant

B. Franklin

P.S. Tuesday Evening.

Since writing the above, I have receiv'd the printed Paper and the Manuscript, containing some Particulars of the Experiment, which I enclose. I hear farther, that the Travellers had perfect Command of their Carriage, descending as they pleas'd by letting some of the inflammable Air [hydrogen] escape, and rising again by discharging some Sand: that they descended over a Field so low as to talk with the Labourers in passing, and mounted again to pass a Hill. The little Balloon falling at Vincennes, shows that mounting higher it met with a Current of Air in a contrary Direction: An Observation that may be of use to future aerial Voyagers.

To Jan Ingenhousz

Dear Friend,   Passy, January 16, 1784

I have this Day received your Favour of the 2d Inst; Every Information in my power respecting the Balloons I sent you just before Christmas, contained in Copies of my letters to Sir Joseph Banks. . . .

It appears as you observe, to be a discovery of great Importance, and what may possibly give a new turn to human Affairs. Convincing Sovereigns of the Folly of Wars, may perhaps be one Effect of it: since it will be impracticable for the most potent of them to guard his Dominions. Five thousand Balloons capable of raising two Men each could not cost more than Five Ships of the Line: And where is the Prince who can afford so to cover his Country with Troops for its Defence, as that Ten thousand Men descending from the Clouds, might not in many places do an infinite deal of mischief before a Force could be brought together to repel them? It is a pity that any national Jealousy, should, as you imagine it may, have prevented the English from prosecuting the Experiment, since they are such ingenious Mechanicians, that in their hands it might have made a more rapid progress towards Perfection, and all the Utility it is capable of affording. . . .   Yours most affectionately

                                                       B. F[ranklin]

58

INDEPENDENCE HAS ITS RESPONSIBILITIES

BEFORE the Revolution American colleges customarily received gifts of money and books from English philanthropists. With the reestablishment of peace in 1783 the trustees of some of these institutions, including Princeton, Columbia, and Dartmouth, sent agents abroad to beg for aid once more. Franklin flatly refused his help in France for reasons he explained in a letter to the president of Princeton. The progress of American institutions was harder and slower without foreign gifts, but it was at least all their own.

To John Witherspoon

Passy, April 5, 1784

Reverend Sir,

I have received the Letter you did me the honour of writing to me the 27th past. It would be a pleasure to me to see you here, but I cannot give you any Expectations of Success in the Project of obtaining Benefactions for your College. Last Year Messrs. Wheelock came hither with the same Views for their College at Dartmouth in New England; and they brought a Recommendation signed by a great Number of the principal People of our States. They apply'd to me for Advice and Assistance, and I consulted some knowing prudent Persons, well acquainted with this Country, and Friends of ours. After well considering the Matter, they gave their Opinion that it was by no means adviseable to attempt a Collection here for such a purpose; for tho' possibly we might get something, it would not be equal to the Expence and Trouble attending the Solicitation; and the very Request would be disgraceful to us, and hurt the Credit of Responsability we wish to maintain in Europe, by representing the United States as too poor to provide for the Education of their own Children. For my own part, I am persuaded we are fully able to furnish our Colleges amply with every Means of public Instruction, and I cannot but wonder that our Legislatures have generally

59

paid so little Attention to a Business of so great Importance. One Circumstance in Messrs. Wheelock's Application here made me somewhat ashamed for our Country. Being ask'd by a Gentleman, what Sums had been subscribed or Donations made by the many eminent Persons who had sign'd the Recommendation, they were not able to say that more than one had given any thing. Meeting with no Encouragement from any other Quarter here, they went to Holland and England. What Success they had in those Countrys, I have not heard. With great Esteem and Respect, I have the honour to be

Reverend Sir,

Your most obedient

and most humble Servant

B. Franklin

FAREWELL

DAVID HARTLEY, an English merchant, inventor, and political figure, had been Franklin's friend for many years. As a member of Parliament he had vigorously opposed the ministerial policies, working earnestly for peace between Great Britain and America both before and during the war. In 1783 a reconstituted ministry sent him to France to conduct the final peace negotiations with the American Commissioners. He signed the definitive Treaty of Peace with the United States on September 3, 1783.

Not until nearly two years later did Congress grant Franklin's request for permission to retire. At last, after eight and a half years of uninterrupted diplomatic service, he was allowed to leave. Seriously ill and in constant pain, he prepared to sail for home. One of his last acts before departure was to write a farewell note to his old friend Hartley in London. It seems a fitting selection from his correspondence with which to close this volume.

To David Hartley

I cannot quit the Coasts of Europe, without taking leave of my ever dear Friend Mr. Hartley. We were long Fellow-Labourers in the best of all Works, the Work of Peace. I leave you still in the Field; but having finish'd my Day's Task, I am going home *to go to Bed*. Wish me a good Night's Rest, as I do you a pleasant Evening. Adieu. And believe me ever

Yours most affectionately

B. Franklin

in his 80th Year.

This volume was printed and bound at
The Lakeside Press, R. R. Donnelley & Sons Company,
Chicago, Illinois, and Crawfordsville, Indiana.
The paper is Mohawk Superfine Text
manufactured by the Mohawk Paper Mills.
The type is Monotype Fournier.
The lettering of the title on the spine is from a set of brass stencils
made for Franklin in 1781 in Paris
and now in the possession of the American Philosophical Society.
The ornamental heading in red on the title page is reproduced from
a stencil for a calling card in the same set.
The cover paper is adapted from the Yale copy of
Franklin's *Pocket Almanack* for 1743.
Color photographs for four of the illustrations
were supplied by *Life* Magazine.
The designers of this volume were Walter Howe
for The Lakeside Press
and Alvin Eisenman
for the Yale University Press.